YOU MUST BE JOKING

IMPROVE YOUR COMMUNICATION, BUSINESS, AND INTERPERSONAL SKILLS, ALL THROUGH THE CORRECT USE OF JOKES.

WRITTEN BY

DARRELL MANGUM

Cover art by Tyson Cole.

ISBN: 9780979460722

CONTENTS

Joke Section A: Ridiculous

Some jokes are beyond explaining. They're just ridiculous. That's why they're funny. People will agonize over these jokes. But it's foolishness to try to understand them. You just go with the ridiculousness of them and let the humor sink in.

A-1

*****

A recently divorced woman moved back to her home town hoping to start over again. While making a dentist appointment she was surprised to see she recognized the dentist's name as a good looking boy from her high school almost 25 years earlier. However, upon walking into the dentist's office, she quickly realized he must be someone else. He was bald, had a big beer belly, and looked a lot older. Just to be sure though, on her way out she asked him if he went to the high school that she had attended.

"Yeah", he responded, "I graduated in 91."

"Oh my gosh", the woman excitedly said "you were in my class."

"Really", he said that's interesting, "what class did you teach?"

A-2

*****

A guy burned both of his ears severely. He called 911 to ask for an ambulance. At the hospital they were asking him how it happened.

He said, "I was ironing my clothing and the phone rang. I got confused, and instead of grabbing the phone, I picked up the iron and burned my ear..."

"But how the heck did you burn the other ear?" The doctor asked.

"How do you think I called you people?"

You might think that the way to deliver this joke is to make the guy with the burned ears sound really stupid. But we already know that. So make his quandary sound very logical.

A-3

*****

Person 1: What's the difference between an elephant and a bag of potatoes?

Person 2: I don't know, what?

Person 1: I'm so never sending you to the store for a bag of potatoes.

A-4

*****

My wife is on a new diet.

Coconuts and bananas.

She hasn't lost weight, but can she climb a tree!

The punch line here should sound as if you've really got something great.

A-5

*****

A librarian is working away at her desk when she notices that a chicken has come into the library and is patiently waiting in front of the desk. When the chicken sees that it has the librarian's attention, it squawks, "Book, book, book, BOOK!"

The librarian complies, putting a couple of books down in front of the chicken. The chicken quickly grabs them and disappears.

The next day, the librarian is again disturbed by the same chicken, who puts the previous day's pile of books down on the desk and again squawks, "Book, book, book, BOOK!"

The librarian shakes her head, wondering what the chicken is doing with these books, but eventually finds some more books for the chicken. The chicken disappears.

The next day, the librarian is once again disturbed by the chicken, who squawks (in a rather irritated fashion, it seems), "Book, book, book, BOOK!"

By now, the librarian's curiosity has gotten the better of her, so she gets a pile of books for the chicken, and follows the bird when it leaves the library.

She follows it through the parking lot, down the street for several blocks, and finally into a large park. The chicken disappears into a small grove of trees, and the librarian follows.

On the other side of the trees is a small marsh. The chicken has stopped on the side of the marsh. The librarian, now really curious, hurries over and sees that there is a small frog next to the chicken, examining each book, one at a time. The librarian comes within earshot just in time to hear the frog saying,

"Read it, read it, read it..."

A-6

*****

A guy ran into his friend, standing on a street corner in the city. This friend was standing there, holding a rope. On the other end of the rope, was an elephant. A real-life, Asian elephant, standing on the sidewalk behind him.

"Good to see ya, buddy!" exclaimed the friend, "Wanna buy this elephant? I'll sell him to you for a thousand dollars!"

This guy was amazed.

“You’ll sell me this elephant for a thousand dollars? What am I going to do with an elephant? I live in a studio apartment on the seventh floor of my building. I have nothing to feed an elephant, and nowhere for him to live. And there you stand, offering to sell me that elephant for a thousand dollars. Are you crazy? That elephant isn’t worth a thousand dollars to me.

I’ll give you five hundred.”

A-7

*****

A man goes to a psychiatrist and says, “Doc, my brother's crazy, he thinks he's a chicken.”

The doctor says, “Why don't you turn him in?”

The guy says, “We would. But we need the eggs.”

Tell this jokes in a steady rhythm, and very seriously. The punch line should sound as if it makes all the sense in the world. Resist the temptation to tell this joke with a crazy affectation.

A-8

*****

A guy with a huge orange head goes in to see a doctor. The doctor says, “How did you get such a huge orange head?”

The guy says, “Well, one day I was walking down the beach when I tripped over an old lantern. A genie came out and said, “I'll grant you three wishes, whatever you desire…what is your first wish?”

I said, “I'd like all the money I could ever spend.”

The genie went Poof!', and there it was, all the money I could ever spend.

Then he said, “What is your second wish?”

I said, "I'd like a beautiful woman to love me, someone I could enjoy this money with."

The genie went Poof! And there she was, a gorgeous girl who immediately loved me.

Then the genie said, "And what is your third wish?'...and I think this is where I went wrong...I said, "I'd like a huge orange head."

A-9

*****

A job applicant is being interviewed.

What is your biggest weakness?

Well, I have a hard time telling reality from fantasy.

And what is your greatest strength?

I'm batman.

Another joke that needs to be told very deliberately and with a very matter-of-fact attitude.

A-10

*****

A guy goes into a flag shop and asks for a green American flag.

"There aren't any green American flags. They only come in red, white and blue."

The guy rubs his chin for a moment and says,

"Okay, then I'll take a blue one."

This joke should be told quickly, and with a hint of frustration in your voice, just like the guy trying to by the flag would have.

A-11

*****

A drunk staggered into a saloon, put his head on the bar, and said, "Give me a scotch."

The bartender said, "Man, you can't even raise your head!"

The drunk said, "Okay, give me a haircut."

A-12

*****

Two muffins are in the oven, cooking.

One muffin turns to the other and says, "Man, it's getting really hot in here."

The other muffin says, "Holy crap! A talking muffin!"

A-13

*****

Three guys, stranded on a desert island, find a magic lantern containing a genie, who grants them each one wish.

The first guy wishes he was off the island and back home.

The second guy wishes the same.

The third guy says "I'm lonely. I wish my friends were back here."

A-14

*****

A penguin walks into a bar, goes to the counter, and asks the bartender, "Have you seen my brother?"

The bartender says, "I don't know. What does he look like?"

A-15

*****

A man tries skydiving.

After a fantastic free fall he pulls the rip cord to open his parachute but nothing happens. He tries everything but can't get it open.

Just then another man comes flying towards him, but he's not falling, he's going UP.

The skydiver yells, "Hey, you know anything about parachutes?"

As the man passes he shouts, "No, you know anything about gas stoves?

A-16

*****

A carpet layer had just finished installing carpet for a lady. He stepped out for a smoke, only to realize he'd lost his cigarettes. In the middle of the room, under the carpet, was a bump. "No sense pulling up the entire floor for one pack of smokes," he said to himself. He proceeded to get out his hammer and flattened the hump.

As he was cleaning up, the lady came in.

"Here," she said, handing him his pack of cigarettes. "I found them in the hallway."

"Now," she said, "if only I could find my gerbil."

A-17

*****

A Labrador went to a telegram office, took out a blank form and wrote, " *Woof. Woof. Woof. Woof. Woof. Woof. Woof. Woof. Woof.*"

The clerk examined the paper and politely told the dog: " *There are only nine words here. You could send another 'Woof' for the same price.*"

"*But,*" the dog replied, "*That would make no sense at all.*"

A-18

*****

A cowboy walks into a wild west saloon, sits down at the bar and asks for a shot of whiskey. The bartender serves him his whiskey and says,

"You hear about the Brown Paper Cowboy? Hung him they did."

The cowboy at the bar looks up and says "Why do they call him the Brown Paper Cowboy?"

The bartender explains, "They call him the Brown Paper Cowboy because all of his clothes are made of brown paper - his hat, his shirt, pants - even his chaps are made of brown paper."

The cowboy nods in recognition and asks, "So why'd they hang him?"

The bartender replies, "Rustlin'."

A-19

*****

Man speaks frantically into the phone, "My wife is pregnant, and her contractions are only two minutes apart!"

"Is this her first child?" the doctor queries.

"No, you idiot!" the man shouts. "This is her husband!"

A-20

*****

A tourist in England walked over to an Englishman and asked,

"Could you tell me where the British Museum is?"

The Englishman said,

"I could."

And then walked on.

A-21

*****

Two nice elderly ladies were sitting together in the coffee shop of a Miami Beach hotel. One asked, “What are your plans for tonight?”

The other said, “I have a date with Al Kemp.”

The first one said, “Al Kemp? He’s an animal! He’ll get you up to his place, tear off your dress, and make love to you! How do you like that?”

The other said, “I’m glad you told me. I’ll wear an old dress.”

A-22

*****

A lawyer is up late one night working on a big case. Suddenly Satan appears and makes an offer. “You can win this case, and every other case you ever try, for as long as you live. In exchange, all I want is your soul, the soul of your mother, your wife, and your children.”

The lawyer considers the offer for a moment and then says,

“So what's the catch?”

A-23

*****

A man calls a lawyer's office. The phone is answered, “Schwartz, Schwartz, Schwartz and Schwartz.” The man says, “Let me talk to Mr. Schwartz.”

“I'm sorry, he's on vacation.”

“Then let me talk to Mr. Schwartz.”

“He's on a big case, not available for a week.”

“Then let me talk to Mr. Schwartz.”

"He's playing golf today."

"Okay, then, let me talk to Mr. Schwartz."

"Speaking."

A-24

*****

The Teacher had asked the class to write an essay about an unusual event that happened during the past week.

Little Johnny got up to read his. It began, "My daddy fell in well last week."

"Good Lord!" the teacher exclaimed. "Is he OK?"

"He must be," said Little Johnny. "He stopped calling for help yesterday."

A-25

*****

A group of high society ladies met for lunch.

One said to the other,

"Oh Mary, those are such beautiful diamonds you're wearing!"

Mary sighed sadly and rolled her eyes.

"They're last year's!"

A-26

*****

At a fine-dining restaurant, the waiter approached a man who was carefully studying the menu. "May I take your order, sir?" he asked.

"Well, I was wondering how you prepare your chicken," The man replied.

"Oh, it's nothing too special, sir," the waiter confided,

"We just tell them straight out they're going to die."

A-27

*****

There were two men working in a construction site.

One of them was in obvious distress and staggering around with his hand to his head. He said to the second guy: "Can you help me find my ear"

The other man dropped to his hands and knees and started searching.

Suddenly he sprang to his feet with a severed ear in his hand and said, "Is this it?"

The other man said, "No, mine has got a pencil behind it."

A-28

*****

A woman went into a famous beauty salon and came out looking twenty years younger.

She told her twenty year old sister all about it.

The sister went and disappeared altogether.

A-29

*****

A drunk guy in Alaska decides to go ice fishing. So he packs up his stuff and goes out onto the ice.

He starts sawing a hole in the ice, and a loud booming voice says, "YOU WILL FIND NO FISH UNDER THAT ICE!"

The drunk looks up, ignores it, and continues on. The voice repeats, "YOU WILL FIND NO FISH UNDER THE ICE."

The drunk looks up and says, "God? Is this God trying to warn me?"

The voice says "NO, I'M THE MANAGER OF THIS ICE RINK."

A-30

*****

A barber was shaving a customer. About ten strokes in, the barber asks,

"Did you have ketchup for lunch?"

The customer answers,

"I haven't had lunch."

"Well, then I think I cut your throat."

A-31

*****

A Boy Scout came to his Scout Leader at camp and said:

"Sir, I found a snake, is it poisonous?"

The Scout Master said: "No camper, this snake isn't poisonous at all!"

The snake bit the boy and the boy immediately starts to spasm and foam at the mouth, leaving the other kids watching, horrified.

The Scout Master continued casually: "However, that snake is venomous. Venom is always injected, while poison is ingested or absorbed through the skin. Let's get it right next time kids."

A-32

*****

There was once a man from the city who was visiting a small farm, and during this visit he saw a farmer feeding pigs in a most extraordinary manner. The farmer would lift a pig up to a nearby apple tree, and the pig would eat the apples off the tree directly. The farmer would move the pig from one apple to another until the pig was satisfied, then he would start again with another pig.

The city man watched this activity for some time with great astonishment.

Finally, he could not resist saying to the farmer,

"This is the most inefficient method of feeding pigs that I can imagine. Just think of the time that would be saved if you simply shook the apples off the tree and let the pigs eat them from the ground!"

The farmer looked puzzled and replied, "What's time to a pig?"

A-33

*****

A guy owned a dog, and claimed that if you gave his dog some money, he would go and buy a newspaper, and bring it back.

The man's friend insisted on a demonstration, so he gave the dog some money and the dog trotted off. An hour later, the dog had not returned.

"How do you explain that?" asked the friend.

"How much money did you give him?"

"Ten dollars."

"Well that explains it. When you give him that much money, he goes to the movies."

A-34

*****

A man enters a barber shop for a shave. While the barber is foaming him up, he mentions the problem he has getting a close shave around his cheeks.

"I have just the thing," says the barber taking a small wooden ball from a nearby drawer. "Just place this between your cheek and gum."

The client places the ball in his mouth and proceeds with the closest shave the man has ever experienced.

After a few strokes, the client asks in garbled speech "And what if I swallow it?"

"No problem" says the barber. "Just bring it back tomorrow like everyone else does!"

A-35

*****

The man being interview was asked:

"What is your greatest strength?"

The man answered:

"I can talk to animals."

"And what is your greatest weakness?"

"Animals can't understand anything I'm saying."

A-36

*****

Two guys are walking side by side down the street. One of them sees a mirror on the ground, grabs it, looks at it, and says, "This guy looks so familiar, but I can't remember where I know him from."

The other guy grabs it from his hand, takes a look at it, and says, "It's me, you idiot!"

A-37

*****

A woman was looking through the frozen turkeys at the supermarket. But she couldn't find one big enough to feed her family. She stopped a stock boy to ask about the turkeys.

"Do these get any bigger?"

The stock boy looked her in the eyes.

"No ma'am. They're dead."

INTRODUCTION

YOU CAN DO IT

I have a good friend that likes to hear me tell a joke. Whenever we're together with other people, at the office or in a party, this friend will encourage me to tell everybody a joke.

I've asked him to tell a joke of his own from time to time, but he won't. He says he just can't do it. He's wrong. Joke telling is just a skill, like playing the piano. You can learn to do it if you want to.

Jokes are everywhere. Everyone tells jokes, everyone hears jokes.

Maybe that's an exaggeration.

I see and hear jokes everywhere, because I'm looking for them. Someone else might say that there are no jokes anywhere. They don't see or hear jokes at all. They're not expecting jokes. They don't notice a joke when it happens right in front of them.

I know people who never tell jokes, and I know people who never seem to understand jokes. I don't like them any less for their attitude about jokes and humor, but I do worry about them. They don't think they need jokes, or they don't like jokes, or they don't understand jokes.

But jokes are still there. Jokes are everywhere. Sometimes jokes are wonderful and will make you laugh hard and stop and think and even change your mood for the day. Other times they will make you groan and roll your eyes. If you've ever told a joke that made people groan, this book might change everything for you. No matter how many times I have heard really bad jokes told, I wouldn't be offering this instruction if I didn't think you could learn to tell jokes.

And remember, it's not the jokes, it's you. You're not telling jokes correctly.

Yes, there are really bad jokes out there.

But the bigger problem is that people don't know HOW to tell jokes.

Telling a joke is a simple thing, it happens all around us all through the day. Comedians on TV tell jokes, our family members and friends tell jokes. I'll wager that we hear dozens of jokes a day, though the art of it seems to elude many people. We might not even recognize a comment is a joke when we hear it. Any time someone says something with the intent of making someone else laugh or smile, they're telling a joke. I watch people attempt to tell a joke and not succeed more often than I hear someone tell a really funny joke. The other side of this equation is the person who frequently makes us laugh just by the things said in common conversation. What makes the difference? Talent? Personality? If you've been told that some people just don't have the talent to tell a joke, don't believe it.

Some people are poor joke-tellers because they haven't learned yet the actual skills required to tell a joke correctly. There are wrong ways, and right ways. There are "do's and don'ts". Some people can figure it out for themselves, and some need proper instruction, like the kind you're reading right now. And don't forget about all the hours of practice that lie ahead. Take this subject seriously. Proper joke telling requires focus and attention to detail.

Are you telling bad jokes? Are you understanding jokes? How do people react when you tell a joke?

Some of you already think you're funny. You think you were born that way. Maybe that's true, and maybe it isn't. You need to understand that there are different kinds of funny. When people say, "That's funny", they might mean:

funny – ha ha, or
funny – clever, or
funny – sniff sniff.

The other side of the coin is that some of you are reading this book because you don't feel funny at all. Your problem isn't telling jokes, it's the jokes themselves. Sometimes you have trouble "getting" jokes that people tell. You listen to someone tell a joke, and you wonder why people are laughing at all.

If you're one of those who has trouble "getting" jokes, don't worry, you're not dumb. Well, not very dumb. And by the way, isn't it interesting that in our culture we've used the word 'dumb' to describe someone who isn't very bright? What does 'dumb' really mean? Maybe those who refuse to speak up and try are the true fools.

Whether or not you're a funny person right now, and whether or not you have a talent right now for telling jokes, you need to know that telling jokes requires confidence. Confidence means speaking up. Confidence means performing. The reality is that when we tell a joke, we're saying to everyone around us, "Hey, look at me! I think I'm funny!"

I have to admit that I worry about people when they try to convince me that they're really funny. Don't convince me, show me.

If I can spend twenty minutes with you, whether or not you tell me a joke I'll know if you're funny, or boring, or annoying, or oblivious. Quick judgment? Sure. But I'm rarely wrong. I hope you're funny. It's enjoyable to sit and visit with someone you can laugh with.

Being funny isn't something that you can explain, and you can't convince someone that you're funny. You either are funny, or you're not. It's just apparent in the things you say and the way that you interact with others. Yes, a lot of people think they're funny, but a lot of people are wrong. If you think you're funny, but the rest of us don't think you're funny, we're going to help you correct your bad habits.

Some people are funny without even trying. At least it seems that way. We appreciate these people. They bring happiness with them wherever they go. Some people light up a room when they come in and always have a smile on their face. They have a witty observation about everything. They're always ready with a funny story or a joke. That's what I love about joke telling. It makes people happy. People who tell good jokes are fun and pleasant people to be around. Joke tellers are friendly, and they inspire confidence.

There are other people who think they are funny, but they aren't. They're just aggressive. They say cruel things about other people and then are the first to laugh at the negative thing they have said. That's nothing like telling a joke. These people will often say that they don't care if this bothers people. I sometimes wonder if they really know that other people in the room fantasize about hitting them with a chair.

All the rest of us have had at least a few bad experiences with joke telling. We've experienced the pain of charity laughs and forced smiles.

We've forgotten how the joke goes right in the middle of the telling. We've gotten the details of the joke wrong. We've failed, and the joke has bombed. Worse than this, some of us have had people mock the jokes we've told. We've been informed that we are not very funny. So we sit quietly and listen to conversation. We're afraid to make a comment or contribute to what's being said.

If you read this book will you learn which of these categories applies to you?

Yes.

Will learn to develop your humor?

Yes.

Will you learn to tell jokes really well and become a truly funny person?

I hope so.

Will you learn to write your own jokes?

I don't know. That's really not the point of this book. I guess I would ask you this: Can you paint a picture? Can you write a song? Can you sculpt a statue? Writing a joke is a lot like all those.

People come up with their own jokes all the time. I'm not sure if that is the same as writing a joke or not, but here's an example of a natural joke from a truly funny person.

Years ago, I was helping out with some community education classes at the local high school. There was a very nice gentleman teaching a computer literacy class. Most of his students were senior citizens who had purchased computers. These folks were thrilled with their new toys, but hadn't the foggiest idea of how to use them or what to do with them.

So the teacher began by asking basic questions about a computer.

"What is a mouse?"

Blank stares.

"What is a monitor?"

Blank stares.

"What is a keyboard?"

Blank stares.

"What is a program?"

No response. This time the teacher answered his own question. He sighed. His head and shoulders slumped, and he said,

"A program is where the teacher goes when the alcohol isn't working anymore."

The computer teacher was a naturally funny man. He made a good joke up, and he did it right on the spot. So you see, jokes and joke telling can become a natural part of your life.

I know that many times in my own life, someone has put me on the spot and asked me to tell a joke. My mind goes blank. I get annoyed.

"I don't know any jokes."

That's an odd thing for me to say, because people know that I collect jokes. Of course it's not true. I know hundreds and hundreds of jokes. People get impatient with me.

"Come on! You're always telling jokes! You give talks about joke telling and humor. You've done standup comedy!"

Sometimes I still draw a blank.

Joke telling is a challenging subject, and many people feel like they don't know any jokes, and sometimes the feel like they don't understand jokes.

Is that you? Do you just not "get it"?

It's not a permanent condition. If you want a better grasp on jokes, it's only a matter of study and practice. Just like learning to play a musical instrument. If you truly are not funny, you can learn to be funny, and you can learn to tell funny jokes.

Writing this book has been a similar experience. I get my notepad, or I get a voice recorder, and I go for a walk, or a ride, or I sit at my computer. Surely there must be something I could say about humor and joke telling.

I got nothing.

I don't know why you can't tell a joke. I don't know why you don't get jokes.

But I must press on. I'm going to try. I'm going to find some things that I can tell you, and hopefully they will help you learn to tell a proper joke. What's the number one piece of advice I would give you?

You have to be your biggest fan.

You have to think that you are funny. Yes, there are many comedians who make a living out of self-deprecation jokes. Self-confidence, courage, belief. Walk into a room knowing that you are going to tell a joke, and people are going to laugh. Believe in yourself. You can do this. You can tell a joke.

Joke Section B: Exaggeration

These jokes are funny because they take simple things, and make a big deal out of them. If you don't understand that, then YOU'RE an exaggeration.

B-1

*****

An elderly Floridian called 911 on her cell phone to report that her car has been broken into. She is hysterical as she explains her situation to the dispatcher:

"They've stolen the stereo, the steering wheel, the brake pedal and even the accelerator!" she cried.

The dispatcher says, "Stay calm, Maam, an officer is on the way."

A few minutes later, the officer radios in.

"Disregard." He says. "She got in the back-seat by mistake."

B-2

*****

If I had only one day left to live, I would live it in my statistics class: it would seem so much longer.

B-3

*****

Bubba was bragging to his boss one day. "You know, I know everyone there is to know. Just name someone, anyone, and I know them."

Tired of his boasting, his boss called his bluff,

Ok, Bubba, how about Tom Cruise?" Sure, yes, Tom and I are old friends, and I can prove it."

So Bubba and his boss fly out to Hollywood and knock on Tom Cruise's door, and sure enough, Tom Cruise shouts, "Bubba! Great to see you! You and your friend come right in and join me for lunch."

Although impressed, Bubba's boss is Still Skeptical. After they leave Cruise's house, he tells Bubba that he thinks Bubba's knowing Cruise was just lucky. No, no, just name anyone else," Bubba says.

"President Obama," his boss quickly retorts.

"Yes," Bubba says, "I know him, let's fly out to Washington." and off they go.

At the white House, Obama spots Bubba on the tour and motions him and his boss over, saying, "Bubba, what a surprise. I was just on my way to a meeting, but you and your friend come on in and let's have a cup of coffee first and catch up."

Well, the boss is very shaken by now, but still not totally convinced. After they leave the white house grounds, he expresses his doubts to Bubba, who again implores him to name anyone else. "The Pope," his boss replies.

"Sure!" says Bubba. "I've known the Pope a long time." So off they fly to Rome. Bubba and his boss are assembled with the masses in Vatican Square when Bubba says, "This will never work. I can't catch the Pope's eye among all these people. Tell you what; I know all the guards so they'll let me just go upstairs and I'll come out on the balcony with the Pope." And he disappears into the crowd headed toward the Vatican.

Sure enough, half an hour later, Bubba emerges with the Pope on the balcony.

But by the time Bubba returns, he finds that his boss has had a heart attack and is surrounded by paramedics. Working his way to his boss' side, Bubba asks him, "What happened?"

His boss looks up and says,

"I was doing fine until you and the Pope came out on the balcony and the Japanese tourist next to me asked, 'Who's that on the Balcony with Bubba????'"

B-4

*****

It was graduation night at the High School and they were about halfway through the ceremony when the principal said, "Ladies and Gentlemen, we have a problem, Pete is a few credits short and won't be able to graduate tonight."

Pete was the quarterback for the football team, and when the student body heard that he wasn't going to graduate, they all jumped up and started to chant, "Give Pete another chance, give Pete another chance!"

The principal announced that they have decided to give Pete another chance. Pete is told that he will be given a "One Question" math test and if he passes, he can graduate.

The question is, "What is 2 plus 3?" Pete thinks for about 20 minutes and finally says, "I have it! The answer is 5!"

There is complete silence in the auditorium for a couple of seconds and then the entire High School football team jumps up and begins to chant, "Give Pete one more chance. Give Pete one more Chance!"

B-5

*****

A prospective tenant wondered about some stains on the walls of the kitchen.

"The man who lived here before," the rental agent said, "was an inventor. He mostly worked with explosives."

"Oh, so those stains are some of the stuff that went wrong?"

"No, those stains are the inventor."

B-6

*****

A guy asked his friend about his trip to Hollywood.

"I hear you met Brad Pitt. Is that true?"

"Did I meet Brad Pitt in Hollywood? How can you even ask that question?"

"Well, I haven't heard about your trip yet."

"Well, let me tell you. I was walking down the street in Hollywood, and I stopped to buy a hotdog from a street vendor. I looked across the street, and there on the balcony of a fancy restaurant sat Brad Pitt eating lunch.

I thought for a minute if I should go over and say hi, but I didn't know what to say. But I just went over anyway and walked up the stairs to the balcony. When I got to Brad's table, I said, 'Hello Mr. Pitt, I'm glad to meet you.' Brad stood up, grabbed my hotdog, shoved it into my mouth, punched me in the face, and pushed me down the stairs to the street."

"So, now you're asking if I met Brad Pitt? Did I meet him? Heck, I had lunch with him!"

B-7

*****

Little Johnny was in math class when the teacher asked the class to solve a problem. The problem was like this:

A rich man worth twenty million dollars dies. One fourth of his wealth goes to his wife, one third to his daughter, and one fifth to his nephew, and the rest is donated to old people's home. Now, what does each party get?"

Little Johnny, sitting on the last bench replied, "A lawyer!"

B-8

*****

A man is walking down a country road and comes across a farmer with a three-legged pig. He asks, "Hey, how'd your pig lose a leg?"

The farmer replies, "Well, let me tell you a story. I was workin' under the tractor when the jack slipped, pinning me under. This here pig ran in, re-set the jack, lifted the tractor up and pulled me to safety."

"Wow," the man said. "So, did the pig have his leg crushed by the tractor? How'd he lose his leg?"

"Well," the farmer said, "Let me tell you another story. My daughter was out back swimming in the cement pond when she started to drown. This here pig dove in the pool, pulled her to safety, called 9-1-1 then gave her mouth-to-mouth until the paramedics arrived."

"Really? That's incredible! Did the pig strain himself while swimming? How did he lose his leg?"

"Well, let me tell you another story. My family and I were sound asleep when the house caught on fire. This here pig rushed in, woke us up, drug my youngest to safety then helped man the fire hoses when the fire department got there."

"No kidding? That's amazing! So, was the pig burned in the fire? How the heck did he lose a leg?"

"Well," the farmer drawled. "Great pig like this, you don't eat 'em all at once."

It makes just as much sense to you and your audience, right?

B-9

*****

A man is carrying on beyond belief at his wife's funeral. No one can console him. He can't be comforted.

"My life is empty. I'm a lost soul!"

A friend put his arm around the man's shoulders.

"What are you talking about? You're a young man! You'll meet another woman. In a year or two you'll get married again."

The man nodded and dabbed at his eyes with his hanky.

"Sure. But what am I going to do tonight?"

B-10

*****

The news reporter asked the one hundred-five-year –old man's advice on how to live to such a ripe old age.

The old man answered, "Nothing to it. Just drink at least one shot of whiskey every day."

"But lots of people drink whiskey every day," the reporter said, "and yet they die long before they reach old age. How do you explain that?"

"Simple," the old man shrugged, "they don't keep doing it long enough."

B-11

*****

Two old maids were reading the obituary column when they noticed that a woman's third husband had died and would be cremated in the morning.

One of the old maids said,

"It's not fair. We can't get one, and some women have husbands to burn!"

B-12

*****

A couple racing to the hospital for the birth of their baby didn't quite make it and the baby was born on the lawn outside the emergency room.

When the bill for the delivery arrived, the young father was upset by one item:

"Delivery room fee: $150.00"

He returned the bill, demanding it be corrected. The baby was born outside on the grass. They never made it to the delivery room.

The revised bill arrived a few days later. It read:

"Green fees: $150.00"

B-13

*****

The airline pilot called to the flight attendant: "Bring me some cotton balls for my ears."

The flight attendant asked: "Captain, does the noise from the engines bother your ears?"

"No," responded the pilot, "But the screaming from the passengers will when I announce that we've lost our landing gear."

B-14

*****

I once met a man who had been married for 50 years.

"Amazing. 50 years!" I said. "What's the secret to such a long, happy marriage?"

"Well," he replied, "It's like this. The man makes all the big decisions… and the woman just makes the little decisions."

"Really?" I responded. "Does that really work?"

"Oh, yes," he said proudly. "50 years, and so far, not one big decision!"

B-15

*****

An old farmer is inconsolable after his dog goes missing. He takes out an ad in the newspaper, but two weeks later, there's still no sign of the mutt.

"What did you write in the ad?" his wife asks.

"'Here, boy,' " he replies.

B-16

*****

Lost in the woods, a hiker spends two days wandering around with no food. Finally, he spots a bald eagle, hits the bird with a big rock and eats it. A park ranger stumbles on the scene and arrests the man for killing an endangered species. In court, the hiker explains that he was on the edge of starvation and had no choice.

"Considering the circumstances, I find you not guilty," says the judge. "But I have to ask—what did the eagle taste like?"

"Well, Your Honor," the hiker replies, "it tasted like a cross between a whooping crane and a spotted owl."

B-17

*****

A talking horse shows up at Dodger Stadium and persuades the manager to let him try out for the team.

In his first at bat, the horse rips the ball deep into right field—then just stands there.

"Run! Run!" the manager screams.

"Run?" says the horse. "If I could run, I'd be in the Kentucky Derby."

B-18

*****

A man said to his friend,

"I don't want you to think I'm a gossip, but people are talking about your wife's inheritance."

The man replied:

"I didn't marry my wife because her father left her half a million dollars.

I'd have married her no matter who left her half million dollars."

B-19

*****

An elderly woman wrote to one of the advice columns:

"I think I made a mistake with my third marriage. My new husband is eighty years old, but he's a sex fiend. He won't leave me alone. He comes after me twenty four hours a day. I could be in the shower, making dinner, or even bending over to turn down the television set. What can I do?

PS. Please excuse the jerky handwriting."

B-20

*****

A doctor sent a dead-beat patient a copy of an overdue bill, saying, "This bill is a year old."

The deadbeat wrote back: "Happy anniversary!"

B-21

*****

A farmer and his brand-new bride were riding home from the chapel in a wagon pulled by a team of horses, when the older horse stumbled.

The farmer said, "That's once."

A little further along, the poor old horse stumbled again.

The farmer said, "That's twice."

After a little, while the poor old horse stumbled again.

The farmer didn't say anything, but reached under the seat, pulled out a shotgun and shot the horse.

His brand new bride yelled, telling him, "That was an awful thing to do."

The farmer said, "That's once."

B-22

*****

Two policemen call the station on the radio.

"Hello, is that you, Sarge?"

"Yes?"

"We have a case here. A woman has shot her husband for stepping on the floor she'd just mopped clean."

"Have you arrested the woman?"

"No sir . . . the floor's still wet."

B-23

*****

A man runs into a friend downtown.

Approaching the friend he comments, “You look terrible. What's the problem?”

“My mother died in June,” he said, “and left me $10,000.”

“Gee, that's tough,” he replied.

“Then in July,” the friend continued, “My father died, leaving me $50,000.”

“Wow. Two parents gone in two months. No wonder you're depressed.”

“And last month my aunt died, and left me $15,000.”

“Three close family members lost in three months? How sad.”

“Then this month,” continued, the friend, “nothing!”

B-24

*****

John walks into his 5th floor apartment after a long day of work, he exhaustively sinks into his favorite armchair, puts up his footrest, turns on the TV, and turns to his wife Hannah, “Honey, please get me a hard drink, I think it’s about to start.”

Hannah rolls her eyes, heads to the kitchen, takes out a beer from the fridge, and brings it to John.

“Honey”, said John, two minutes later, “please get me another one quickly before it starts.”

“WHAT THE HELL IS WRONG WITH YOU, YOU LAZY GOOD FOR NOTHING!” Hannah exclaimed, “DO YOU THINK I’M YOUR PERSONAL WAITER!? YOU PLOP YOURSELF DOWN ON YOUR EASY CHAIR AND EXPECT ME TO BE ON YOUR BECK AND CALL!? IS THAT ALL I’M GOOD FOR!?

John sighs, and mutters under his breath, “it started….”

B-25

*****

Patient: "Doctor, Doctor... I can't stop stealing things".

Doctor: "Take these pills for a week. If that doesn't work, bring me a 50 inch TV".

B-26

*****

An army colonel retired and took along the orderly who had worked for him for twenty years. The colonel told the orderly that his job would be just the same as it had been in the army. The first morning in civilian life the orderly entered the colonel's room and woke him. Then the orderly slapped the colonel's wife and said,

"Okay honey, it's back to town for you!"

B-27

*****

An engineer dies and reports to the pearly gates. St. Peter checks his dossier and says, "Ah, you're an engineer ... you're in the wrong place."

So, the engineer reports to the gates of hell and is let in.

Pretty soon, the engineer gets dissatisfied with the level of comfort in hell, and starts designing and building improvements. After a while, they've got air conditioning, flush toilets and escalators; the engineer soon becomes a pretty popular guy.

One day, God calls Satan up on the telephone and says with a sneer: "So, how's it going down there in hell?"

Satan replies: "Hey, things are going great! We've got air conditioning, flush toilets, and escalators! And there's no telling what this engineer is going to come up with next!"

God exclaims: "What? You've got an engineer? That's a mistake! He should never have gotten down there; send him up here."

Satan, standing his ground, challenges: "No way. I like having an engineer on the staff, and I'm keeping him."

God replies threateningly: "Send him back up here or I'll sue!"

Satan laughs uproariously and answers: "Yeah, right! And just where are YOU going to find a lawyer?"

B-28

*****

During an anti-harassment seminar at work, I asked, "What's the difference between harassment and good-natured teasing?"

A co-worker shouted, "A million dollars."

B-29

*****

A man working with an electric saw accidentally cuts off all of his fingers. At the emergency room, his doctor says, "Give me the fingers, and I'll see what I can do."

The injured man replies, "But I don't have the fingers!"

"Why didn't you bring them?" the doctor asks.

The injured man responds, "Doc, I couldn't pick them up."

B-30

*****

Two guys were talking in a park one day:

"I'm not going back to work until my boss takes back what he said to me."

"What did he say?"

"He said, 'You're fired!'"

B-31

*****

Two tourists went into a roadside diner. When the waitress came over, one man said,

"I'd like some coffee with milk and sugar."

The second man said,

"I'd like the same, but could you make sure the cup is clean?"

A few minutes later the waitress came back with their coffees and asked,

"Okay, which of you gets the clean cup?"

B-32

*****

A new bride on her honeymoon jumped into the bed and snuggled up to her husband.

"Sweetheart," She said. "Is it true that we can do anything we want now that we're married?"

The new husband smiled a devious smile.

"Yep. That's true. We can do anything we want."

"Anything?"

"Anything!"

"Then I'm going to sleep."

B-33

*****

A man was drowning just off shore. He yelled, "Help! I can't swim! I can't swim!"

And old man on the beach hollered back.

"Simmer down! I can't swim either, but you don't see me making a fuss about it!"

B-34

*****

A priest, a minister and a guru sat discussing the best positions for prayer while a telephone repairman worked nearby. “Kneeling is definitely the best way to pray,” the priest said.

“No,” said the minister. “I get the best results standing with my hands outstretched to Heaven.”

“You're both wrong,” the guru said. “The most effective prayer position is lying down on the floor.”

The repairman could contain himself no longer. “Hey, fellas,” he interrupted, “The best praying I ever did was when I was hanging' upside down from a telephone pole.”

B-35

*****

A failing zoo was desperate for a new attraction to bring in more visitors. Unable to afford more animals, the zoo manager persuaded a worker to dress up as a gorilla.

The worker really gave it his all and people believed he was actually a gorilla. He ate bananas, swung from branches and ropes, and beat his chest with great vigor.

But one day he got carried away and fell into the lion exhibit next door.

“Help! Help!” cried the fake gorilla.

The lion let out a great roar and rushed at the worker in the gorilla costume. He knocked him over and stood with his paws on the gorilla’s chest and growled a low growl.

“Quiet down, or we’ll both lose our jobs.

B-36

*****

Bill was in his office, struggling with an account. He asked his secretary for some mathematical help.

"If I were to give you $20,000, less 14%, how much would you take off?" he asked her.

The secretary replied, "Everything but my earrings."

B-37

*****

A man is being sentenced for murdering his wife. The judge banged his gavel.

"You have been found guilty of beating your wife to death with a wrench."

There was a shout from the public gallery.

"You monster!"

The judge banged his gavel again.

"You have also been found guilty of beating your wife's lover to death with a wrench."

A shouting voice arose again from the public gallery.

"You monster! You dirty rotten, no good monster!"

The judge banged his gavel louder and called out to the man.

"I understand your outrage at these horrible crimes, but I will not tolerate another outburst."

"I'm sorry, your honor", the man explained. "But I've lived next door to this man for fifteen years, and every time I ask to borrow a wrench, he says he doesn't have one."

Chapter One

Why

"I don't get it."

If you're telling jokes, you'll hear this all the time.

"I don't get it."

I know you've even said it yourself. I've said it more than I'd like to admit.

If we don't 'get it', does that mean we're stupid?

Yes.

I'm afraid it does.

It's just a joke, after all. It's not the KFC's secret chicken recipe.

Being stupid, not getting jokes, is caused by a number of things.

Not paying attention.

If you weren't listening, just say so. But remember, a joke only lasts a minute or two. Sometimes even less.

Surely your attention span is longer than that.

Or.

You're just not thinking.

Where did he say the salesman was from? How many chickens were there? What color were the lady's eyes? Were you listening to the details of the joke?

I hate to tell you this, but one of the BEST things about jokes is the kick I get when people don't get it.

Maybe I'm being a little harsh.

Maybe the joke references things that you just simply aren't familiar to you.

But, then again, maybe your problem is that you think that jokes are simple and stupid.

They're not.

Jokes are very intelligent, and they make a powerful comment on culture and society.

A famous philosopher once said that a workable life philosophy could be composed entirely of jokes.

Pay attention.

Think about it.

Work it over in your head.

Realize that the joke teller is TRYING to be funny.

If all else fails ask somebody to explain it to you.

But remember: Jokes lose everything if someone has to explain them.

So what's the deal with all these jokes?

Is it really important to know how to tell a joke?

Why are some jokes funny, and other jokes are not?

What is funny?

Who gets to decide?

Obviously I think I know, because I'm trying to explain it to you. Am I going to be successful? Some would say it's a fool's errand.

Mark Twain said, "Explaining humor is a lot like dissecting a frog, you learn a lot in the process, but in the end the frog dies."

I guess it's true to say that I'm going to try to explain jokes and humor. But I'm not trying to make you laugh, so I'm not as worried about killing humor as I would normally be if I were just telling jokes with friends.

Let's go back to the beginning of humor.

Where do jokes come from?

I believe that many jokes come from real life. They are true incidents, observations, and stories that are shortened and exaggerated over time. I think that some jokes develop from actual occurrences, or things that people can see potentially occurring. Other jokes are based on ridiculous scenarios, and we'll talk about them later.

Misunderstandings are funny. Movies are full of misunderstandings. Jerry scratches his cheek, but the girl in the car next to him thinks she saw him pick his nose. You said "six", but your mom thought you said "sex". We'll talk more about misunderstandings later. But they are almost always funny and material for jokes.

The other thing about humor, is the fact that it is the truth. We laugh at things that are true. Even difficult things. If a comedian tells political jokes, and everybody laughs, it's because of the truth in the jokes. Even if you are offended by those jokes, they are still true. That's why we either laugh or are offended. If I make jokes about how fat a politician is, and the truth is that the politician is skinny, then my joke isn't funny. The truth is always funny to most people who hear it.

Most jokes that you hear casually are alterations of older jokes. There's a famous saying that says, "There is nothing new under the sun". It's true. Most of the jokes I hear, and most of the jokes that I have studied and searched, are old jokes. I see them over and over again. Older books have language that matches the lingo of the day. Very, very few jokes are original in any way.

So we've got jokes to learn and tell, and that's a good thing. But there's no guarantee that your sense of humor is going to be running at full potency when you tell your new jokes. What can we do about that? Let's take some time and dive a little deeper into the subject of humor. This is my favorite part, because people think I'm funny, and I think I'm funny. It's also the thing about me I like most. It's fun to be funny. And it's not just a matter of opinion. I've had plenty of opportunities to prove that I'm funny, to myself and others.

Does this mean I'm always telling jokes? Sure! I love to tell jokes. But I love to find opportunities to make people laugh with any kind of funny comment.

Have I been one hundred percent successful?

No.

I've had plenty of people sneer at me and say: "What! Do you think you're funny or something?"

Yes, I think I'm funny, but I'm not a stranger to telling a joke and having it fail. I admit that it doesn't happen very often, but I'm not afraid to tell you that once in a while, I tell a joke that bombs. Why have my jokes or funny comments failed? Maybe I chose the wrong time to tell a joke. No one was paying attention. Maybe I picked the wrong audience.

Humor is a real part of our society and a real part of our daily lives. Humor is everywhere, even at a funeral. Why is it important? Humor is like a big mirror. Humor reflects back to us things about ourselves, our communities, and our situations that are noteworthy. What are all things that are happening around us? What's so funny? We are! We are funny. It's in the way that we react to the things that happen to us. Humor is in the way we live our lives. Maybe it's funny when we live carefree and haphazardly. Maybe it's funny when we take ourselves too seriously.

When we listen to a comedian, when we see a funny movie, or when a friend tells a joke, we listen and see ourselves in the humor. We laugh because the humor is familiar. Maybe the person in the joke is really stupid. That doesn't mean we are exactly like the stupid person, but we can identify enough with the situation of the joke, that we understand enough to laugh. We've all felt stupid before. We all have a mother-in-law or a stupid brother, or an annoying neighbor.

Is this way of thinking always healthy? There are definitely lines that are frequently crossed. If you like really stupid jokes, or vulgar jokes, that says a lot about the image you see in the humor mirror.

I recently watched a movie with my extended family. A dear family member, who watch the majority of our group laughing hysterically at this funny movie, whispered to me secretly: "I don't think I have a sense of humor."

I felt so bad for her. We've spent a good amount of time in the past couple of weeks talking about humor and her own personal struggle with it. Some of what we'll talk about in this book was very useful and pertinent to this family member of mine.

Appreciating humor is one thing, being funny is another. No, you don't have to become the class clown or a stand-up comedian to get the most out of this book, but I want you to understand what goes into learning to be a funny person. I'll show you how humor can benefit almost any part of your life. It helps in sales situations, humor lightens up a dreary business meeting, jokes make family visits memorable, and I've even seen priceless humor brighten hearts at a funeral.

Yes, humor can be taken to an extreme, and that's never good. Some people make jokes about sensitive things. Some people joke about the appearance of others and choose things that the person can't change. Some make jokes about the beliefs of others. Whether or not you choose to go there is up to you. All of our actions bring consequences, and if you choose to use jokes to mock others you will reap the negative rewards.

Is being funny a scientific thing? What analogy can we use to explain a good joke? I like to compare a good joke to a sporting event. That's because joke telling takes real effort, and you will either win or lose. But is a joke like a golf putt, or a basketball free throw? It can't be as difficult as I'm describing here, right? Wrong. Jokes take the concentration of a golf putt or a basketball free throw.

Seems like joke telling shouldn't be that hard. There's nothing difficult or tricky about being funny. Right? A lot of people think that they are funny.

A lot of people are wrong.

I mean, I can play chopsticks on the piano. I can play chopsticks perfectly. Does that mean I can play the piano?

But you and me, we're funny enough, aren't we? I'm talking about all us joke-tellers. Do we have to act like foolish clowns to tell a funny joke? We can, but we don't have to. We're just funny. Some of you are dignified, with an accent of cute or witty. If you're not funny, silly or ridiculous at all, it's because you're just more serious and mature than all those clowns out there thinking that they are sooo funny. Besides, being funny is a sign of immaturity and a lack of responsibility, right?

Wrong.

Most of us would like to add a little more humor to our lives, most of us would like for people to laugh at the things we say, but few of us even know how to begin. Oh, we'd like to think we know how humor works, but that driving question still lingers in the back of our minds: "Is this funny, or is it just stupid?"

Being funny is not stupid. In fact, it's just the opposite. Some of the smartest people I ever met were also some of the funniest. I think intelligence and humor are very connected.

Just remember, you shouldn't have to try too hard to be funny. Humor should flow naturally. Forced humor sounds lame. And yet, if you work when you're NOT in front of an audience, you'll develop tools and skills that will strengthen your funny bone. Yes, you'll have to work and try, but it's fun work. It's entertaining. Practice and try, and let the humor flow naturally.

Sometimes trying too hard to be funny has negative effects. Trying too hard to be funny makes us annoying or turns people into bullies. It's tempting to try too hard. It can be a little thrilling to watch someone cringe or cower or stagger because of something funny we said about them. Cruel comments and abusive practical jokes are a sign of severe insecurity. Be careful with humor, it's a very powerful thing.

The other thing that's tempting about trying to be funny, is that there are so many pleasant rewards. People laugh at our jokes when we're successful. We feel popular. It's nice to be funny, and it's probably funny to be too nice. Some people think that being funny exclusively means being rude to others. But I'm here to teach you that you can infuse your jokes with all the niceness you want. First let's talk about the how's and do's and don'ts of funny.

We all know someone who is truly funny. What is it about them that makes them special? Are they kind, or aggressive? Smart or stupid? Does it seem natural, or learned? Could you learn to be funny like them? I think that most people could be funny if they had some basic training. Many people are funny, but don't seem to know it.

Always remember that being funny doesn't include being stupid. (unless stupid is part of the joke) Wrong approaches to humor will be discussed later.

My first instruction is this: lighten up. Maybe it's silly to be funny, and maybe it's funny to be silly. Humor means not taking yourself, others and most situations so seriously.

A minute ago, I was comparing humor to games. Being funny is a lot like playing golf.

Golfers walk along, enjoying the great outdoors. Most of what they do is walking. They walk from shot to shot. They are preparing for that shot, they are thinking about that shot, but they're mostly walking to get to the next shot.

Once the golfer gets to the shot, it's not always going to be a great shot. With luck most of the shots will be good enough. Sadly, too many of them will be bad shots, and frustrating shots.

A great joke or a truly funny moment is like a great golf shot. It's a moment that you can enjoy as you watch it happen. But just as in golf, where even professionals say that great shots are rare, truly funny moments are infrequent. That's what makes them so wonderful. You'll have more moments of stupid jokes and mildly amusing comments. Shrug your shoulders and grin. That makes you a pleasant person, which I believe is more important than being funny.

And I asked before, is a joke like a free throw? Sure it is. You line yourself up, and you give it your best shot. If you've done some practicing, you have a good idea if you're going to be close or not. The trick is to keep shooting. Keep practicing. You'll get better and better.

If you think that everything you say is funny, if you long to be the center of attention, if you feel like you're "The Life of The Party," you've got some things to learn that we'll be discussing shortly, and there's a possibility that you're going to be embarrassed as we discover how wrong you are.

There's another extreme we haven't addressed. Some people don't want anything at all to do with jokes and humor. Some people think that being funny is not dignified. They feel that joke telling simply isn't for educated, well-mannered people. They do not think that humor could enhance any part of their life in any way. I can understand their point of view. They have probably met a lot of people who considered themselves funny, and weren't. They were just annoying. They were embarrassing and offensive and silly looking.

You know these people too. They are uptight, and rigid, and stuffy.

Actually, I think that there are people who exist just fine without telling jokes or involving themselves in frivolous humor. Some people do well with a very serious personality. They are stoic, use few words, don't smile much, and never joke. And it works for them. These people are John Wayne and Senator Mitch McConnell.

Those who don't see value in humor miss some very important points. Humor gives a special insight into politics, religion, and culture.

Ludwig Wittgenstein said: A serious and good philosophical work could be written consisting entirely of jokes. Very true. There are books of satire about very serious subjects, like religion and politics.

People who have been turned off to being funny by these brash attempts at humor, spend the balance of their tense lives trying hard to give an appearance of sobriety and down-to-earthiness. You can easily spot these people in a crowd, they have a permanent look on their face that says, "I don't get it." These people don't want to "get it." Humor is beneath them.

But humor isn't undignified. Funny people are very valuable in our society. Funny people often have funny things to say, even when they don't feel very funny inside. They do this because they know that it will save them from becoming crotchety old people someday. And we all know that some people become crotchety old people, even in many cases by the age of thirty.

What else does joke telling have to offer?

Many people struggle with communication skills. In the workplace, among friends and in families, they have a hard time getting important information to other people. I know you've experienced this before.

Have you ever listened to someone struggle to talk in a business setting? The speaker has important information that they are trying to share. But their presentation is boring. They mumble. Their speaking pattern is monotone. The information doesn't flow. The speaker drones on and on at times, and then only lightly touches other points that seem important. The presentation of information seems random and goes nowhere. Soon, nothing the speaker is saying makes sense. No one seems to know what the point of it all is.

If the speaker knew how to tell a joke, then he would understand that his audience needs a picture in their minds of the information being shared. They need a set up. They need to understand quickly what the point is. They need the speaker to follow a path that will lead them to a great pay-off of something they need to know.

A speaker would learn to share information effectively from learning to tell jokes. Even if the only skill acquired is just the courage to speak up in front of other people and say what you have to say, learning to tell jokes is the way to build the skill.

All information has a setup and a punch line. Whether it's a report to the board of directors, or a sermon at church, the information has a point, and information that supports that point. That's what a joke has. If you can learn to deliver a joke effectively, you can learn to deliver any information effectively.

Jokes require you to remember and transmit important information so that it can be easily understood and associated.

Jokes teach you to think on your feet. Especially if you're improvising your own humor. Dealing with a heckler, or anticipating how an audience will react, all these things give you powerful skills to use when you have to address an audience with any kind of information.

Learning to tell jokes properly will help you develop many skills.

For example: I'm bilingual. I speak Spanish. I spent time living with my wife's family for a few years, and I learned Spanish. I'm proud of that. One of the most impactful ways of learning a new language came from having children teach me jokes. I wanted so much to learn jokes in Spanish. I wanted to tell them correctly. I wanted to understand them. I needed to pronounce ever word correctly. I needed to enunciate each phrase and sentence correctly, delivering the correct inflection and implication. I needed to understand the double meanings of words and the reasons why the jokes were funny.

No one expected me to tell jokes in Spanish, and they always roared with laughter when I did. And more importantly, my Spanish was very, very good. And it was in large part because of learning to tell jokes in Spanish.

You've probably heard most of the jokes in this book before. I don't expect that anyone will think that these jokes are new or original. That's not the point. How you tell them is more important than whether or not they're new.

We alter jokes to fit situations and places. Any information you might share that is important would benefit by being presented in a way that is relevant to your audience. That's the way we tell jokes. You might have heard one or more of the jokes in this book told in a different way. It doesn't matter. You might have heard that a lawyer did such and such, or a blonde, or whomever. Or the joke might have happened in Texas, or Boston, or Canada. The important thing is to tell a joke about people and occurring in places that will make your audience perk up and listen.

Jokes are pertinent, or at least they should be. They should capture a moment. They can ease tension. They give insight into politics and current events. If you tell a joke that has no point of reference that your audience can understand, your joke will seem lame even if it truly is funny. So you can change the joke you're telling. Make it happen in a place and time that your audience will understand. Make it happen to people that your audience can relate to.

Jokes are best when they seem improvised. That means making a joke sound like you're making it up on the spot. A joke isn't like a classical piano concert. A joke really sounds stale if it seems to be heavily practiced. Right now, this might sound confusing. It's ironic that you should avoid telling your jokes as if they were heavily practiced, because I'm going to ask you to practice joke telling. Even though you are going to learn, memorize and practice your jokes, they should never sound learned, practiced and memorized.

The holy grail of jokes are the jokes that are invented on the spot to highlight a given event or situation. Sometimes these great jokes are called quips. People who can quip or tell good jokes seem to be smart and sophisticated and important. They casually and effectively drop a quip or a joke into the material they are presenting.

So, we've talked about how jokes help us communicate, but we still don't have a conclusion about humor and what it means. What's funny? Who gets to decide?

Well, everyone and no one gets to decide. Different things are funny to different people. But most people haven't got a clue. They'll laugh just because everyone else is laughing, and they don't want to feel left out. Still, there are some ideas that guide us in understanding exactly what is funny.

All humor contains an element of cruelty. Most of the time we're laughing at someone's expensive, even if that person is imaginary. Jokes draw attention to the stupid, the confused, and the disadvantaged. If you don't get it, you're on their side. Humor is exclusive. You're in, or you're out. You get it, or you don't. That's the pleasure of humor. When we get it, when we're laughing, it means that we understand, and we're part of the group. There's a difference between thinking something is funny, and simply understanding the point of the allegedly funny thing that has been said.

Unexpected things are funny. Something we didn't expect grandma to say. A mistake the pastor made at the pulpit last Sunday.

It's hard to believe, but hard things we go through teach us to be funny. There's humor in almost all the bad things we suffer.

True things are funny. Comedians on TV make comments about current events that are absolutely true.

Irreverent things are funny. There are great jokes about death and divorce and poverty and criminals.

Some people will view comedy that is pretty universally accepted as funny and tell you they think it's stupid. Everybody else thinks the comedy is funny, and this person thinks it's stupid. Even if they understand the point of the joke, their eyebrows narrow, and they grimace to express their distaste. Why does this happen? It is possible that this is because everyone has different tastes. They may understand the point the comedy is trying to make, but they simply don't find it funny. But I have to be honest. It has been my experience that often when people tell you they think a certain joke or comedy routine is stupid, the truth is that they simply don't get it.

It's not because the comedy is too intelligent, but more likely because the listener is too uptight. Or too dense. I asked my dad to name his favorite Marx brothers routine, and he told me that the Marx brothers were stupid. My children and I had been enjoying a collection of Marx brother's routines on DVD, so we brought them over to watch with my dad. As my dad watched, I observed him. I could see that he was totally oblivious to the humor. He didn't understand where Groucho and Harpo and Chico were coming from. He didn't understand their references, he didn't understand their double meanings. The whole thing was just flying by him without any understanding at all.

My dad wasn't ignorant, he just wasn't trying. He didn't care, so he wasn't paying attention.

Some people will only laugh when humor hits them in the face like a giant snowball. They see someone fall down, or smack a guy across the face. They don't have to think about what makes it funny. But true humor requires that we pay attention and think about what's happening and what is being said.

Humor uses references and allusions. This creates exclusivity. If someone says something funny about the local mayor, and you know nothing about the mayor, you're not going to understand why everyone is laughing. You'll be on the outside looking in.

Sometimes people don't understand the references and allusions and laugh anyway. People laugh because of peer pressure.

Before I was married, I tried my hand at stand-up comedy. There was a club in Salt Lake City that had amateur night on Tuesdays, and a club in Provo that had amateur night on Wednesdays. I would take fifteen minutes each night. I did the same routine each time. I had practiced for weeks and could have recited the jokes in my sleep.

But an interesting thing would happen night to night. I would always be introduced as an amateur comic in almost a disposable way.

"Hey folks! Here's a new guy, he's just starting out, he's an amateur, he's only done this a couple of times, so please give him a chance, okay?"

That's what was said as I was taking the stage. Sometimes the audience would give me their full attention and laugh and laugh. That felt great! Other nights they would ignore me, and no one would laugh. People would chat at their tables or take time to order food and drinks. That was really hard.

So I told the comedian who was hosting the show one night about my dilemma. He immediately understood the reason.

"People don't laugh at jokes because they are funny. They laugh because everyone else is laughing."

I wasn't buying it, so he told me he would demonstrate. When it was my turn to go on, the host began to talk about me.

"This next performer is a close friend of mine. His career is just skyrocketing! I'm as happy for his success as he is! He's just finished a month of sold-out engagements in Chicago and now he's on his way to California to appear on a national talk show, and I convinced him to stop and share his show with us here tonight!"

The audience erupted in applause. They came to their feet as I walked onto the stage. The host gathered me up in a big bear hug. I couldn't even start my jokes until the audience stopped clapping and settled down.

After that the audience laughed like crazy at absolutely everything I said. They even laughed at filler stuff that they weren't supposed to laugh at. It felt wonderful! My mind felt alive with funny things to say. I had never felt so clever. People were wiping away tears and holding their sides. It was like a huge storm of laughter for thirty minutes. When I finished, I got a very wlong standing ovation. As I walked off the stage, the host gave me a big bear hug and whispered to me,

"See what I mean? They don't know what funny is, they just want to feel like they've chosen something popular.

Why did the audience laugh? Was I really funnier that night than I had been before?

Certainly not.

I seemed funnier to that audience because someone of authority told them that I was funny and instructed them to laugh.

Unbelievable? It's true. How does this apply to your joke telling from now on? You're going to learn the power of setting up a joke, and applying some self-confidence.

JOKE SECTION C: SURPRISE

These jokes are funny because your audience won't expect the punchline. It's falls on them totally out of the blue.

C-1

*****

An elderly husband and wife visit their doctor when they begin forgetting little things. Their doctor tells them that many people find it useful to write themselves little notes. When they get home, the wife says,

"Dear, will you please go to the kitchen and get me a dish of ice cream? And maybe write that down so you won't forget?"

"Nonsense," says the husband, "I can remember a dish of ice cream."

"Well," says the wife, "I'd also like some strawberries and whipped cream on it."

"My memory's not all that bad," says the husband. "No problem — a dish of ice cream with strawberries and whipped cream. I don't need to write it down."

He goes into the kitchen; his wife hears pots and pans banging around. The husband finally emerges from the kitchen and presents his wife with a plate of bacon and eggs.

She looks at the plate and asks, "Hey, where's the toast I asked for?"

C-2

*****

A young man asked an old rich man how he made his money.

The old guy fingered his expensive wool vest and said, "Well, son, it was 1932. The depth of the Great Depression. I was down to my last nickel."

"I invested that nickel in an apple. I spent the entire day polishing the apple and, at the end of the day, I sold the apple for ten cents."

"The next morning, I invested those ten cents in two apples. I spent the entire day polishing them and sold them at 5:00 pm for 20 cents. I continued this system for a month, by the end of which I'd accumulated a fortune of $9.80."

"Then my wife's father died and left us two million dollars."

C-3

*****

A tourist is picked up by a cabbie in New York on a dark night. The passenger taps the driver on the shoulder to ask him something. The driver screams, loses control of the car, nearly hits a bus, drives up on the sidewalk, and stops inches from a shop window.

For a second everything went quiet in the cab, then the driver said, "Look friend, don't EVER do that again. You scared the daylights out of me!"

The passenger apologizes and says he didn't realize that a "little tap" could scare him so much. The driver, after gathering himself together replied,

"Sorry, it's not really your fault. Today is my first day as a cab driver - I've been driving hearses for the last 25 years!"

C-4

*****

A guy meets a pirate in a bar. The pirate has a peg-leg, a hook and an eye patch.

"How'd you end up with a peg-leg?" asks the man.

"I was swept overboard in a storm," says the pirate. "A shark bit off me whole leg."

"Wow!" Said the seaman. "What about the hook?"

"We were boarding an enemy ship, battling the other sailors with swords. One of them cut me arm right off."

"Incredible!" remarked the man. "And the eye patch?"

"A seagull dropping fell in me eye," replied the pirate.

"You lost your eye to a seagull dropping?" the man asked incredulously.

Said the pirate: "It was the first day with the hook."

C-5

*****

As I was packing for my business trip, my 3 year old daughter was having a wonderful time playing on the bed.

At one point, she said, "Daddy, look at this," and stuck out two of her fingers. Trying to keep her entertained, I reached out and stuck her tiny fingers in my mouth and said, "Daddy's gonna eat your fingers!" pretending to eat them before I rushed out of the room again.

When I returned, my daughter was standing on the bed staring at her fingers with a devastated look on her face.

I said, "What's wrong, honey?"

She replied, "What happened to my booger?

C-6

*****

Three weeks after her wedding day, Joanna called her minister. "Reverend," she wailed, "John and I had a DREADFUL fight!"

"Calm down, my child," said the minister, "it's not half as bad as you think. Every marriage has to have its first fight!"

"I know, I know!" said Joanna. "But what am I going to do with the BODY?"

C-7

*****

I was visiting my daughter and son-in-law last night when I asked if I could borrow a newspaper.

"This is the 21st century, old man," he said.

"We don't waste money on newspapers. Here, you can borrow my iPad."

After a minute I gave it back and said "Let me tell you, that fly never knew what hit it...."

C-8

*****

There was a new bartender in town. One night, a man ran into the bar and screamed

"RUN FOR YOUR LIVES, BIG JAKE IS COMIN'!"

Everybody ran out the door shrieking in fear, except the terrified bartender.

An enormous man with more tattoos than skin stalks into the bar.

He says, "I'll take a vodka. Now!"

The petrified bartender hands him the bottle. He drains it, and then eats the shot glass, followed by the bottle. The bartender, quivering in fear, says "Would you…would you like anything else?"

The hulking brute says "No thanks. I've got to get out of here. Didn't you hear? Big Jake is comin'!"

This joke requires some acting. You have to portray the big guy as mean and threatening at first, and then afraid of Big Jake in the punch line.

C-9

*****

A little girl received two gifts for her birthday and just couldn't stop talking about them. Finally her mother couldn't stand to hear about it anymore and said:

"Now listen, we're having company for dinner, and it isn't nice to boast about your belongings in front of people. Please don't mention your singing dolly or your new perfume at the table!"

The little girl sat squirming but quiet during the meal. But when her mother stepped out to the kitchen, the child said quietly, "If anybody smells anything, it's me."

C-10

*****

A hunter walking through the jungle was surprised to find a pygmy standing beside a very large dead beast…

Amazed, he asked, "Did you kill that?"

The pygmy answered, "Yes."

The hunter then asked, "How could a little guy like you kill a huge beast like that?"

Said the pygmy, "I killed it with my club."

The astonished hunter asked, “How big is your club?”

The pygmy replied, “There's about 60 of us.”

Tell this one in a very serious, very dry, very matter-of-fact way. Don't overdo the punch line.

C-11

*****

On their first date, Joe took Rose to the carnival. When he asked her what she wanted to do first, Rose replied, “Get weighed.”

So Joe took her to the man with the scale who guesses people's weight. He looked at Rose and said, “One hundred and twenty pounds.” Since Rose weighed in at one seventeen, she collected a prize.

Next they went on the roller coaster. When the ride was finished, Joe asked Rose what she wanted to do next. “Get weighed,” she said. So they went back to the man with the scale, who of course guessed Rose's weight correctly.

Leaving without a prize, they went for a ride on the merry-go-round. After they got off, Joe asked Rose what she wanted to do next. “I want to get weighed!” she said again.

Joe began to think this girl was quite strange, and decided to end the evening quickly. He left her at the door with a quick handshake.

Rose's roommate was waiting up for her to return and asked how the evening went.

“Wousy!” Rose replied.

C-12

*****

Three elderly sisters, Mary, Martha and Betsy in a house together. One night

Mary draws a bath. She puts her foot in and pauses. She yells to the other sisters, "Was I getting in or out of the bath?"

The Martha yells back, "I don't know. I'll come up and see."

She starts up the stairs and pauses. Then she yells to Betsy "Was I going up the stairs or down?" Betsy is sitting at the kitchen table having tea listening to her sisters. She

shakes her head and says, "I sure hope I never get that forgetful, knock on wood."

She then yells, "I'll come up and help both of you as soon as I see who's at the door."

C-13

*****

Mr. Gable had a leak in the roof over his dining room, so he called a repairman to take a look at it.

"When did you first notice the leak?" the repairman inquired.

Mr. Gable scowled. "Last night, when it took me two hours to finish my soup!"

C-14

*****

Bob and Earl were best friends and had been for 50 years. They went to baseball games together and had the best time possible. They truly loved the game but they always wondered if there was baseball in heaven and agreed that whoever died first had to call the other guy and tell them if there was baseball in heaven.

Then one night Earl died. A few days later Bob went to Earl's funeral and came home after the burial service. Then the phone rang and it was Earl.

Earl said, "Bob is this you?"

Bob said, "Yes, Earl how are you doing and is there baseball in heaven?"

Earl said, "Well I've got some good news and some bad news."

Bob said, "What's the good news?"

Earl said, "Well there is baseball in heaven and you can play with Babe Ruth and everybody its great."

Bob said, "Then what's the bad news?"

Earl said, "Well Bob, you're pitching tomorrow night!"

C-15

*****

One day a secretary is leaving on her lunch break, and she notices her boss standing in front of a shredder with a clueless look on his face. The secretary walks up to him and asks if he needs help.

"Yes!" he says looking and sounding relieved, "This is very important."

Glad to help, she turns the shredder on and inserts the paper.

Then her boss says, "Thanks, I only need one copy."

C-16

*****

A man takes his Rottweiler to the vet and says,

"My dog's cross-eyed, is there anything you can do for him?"

"Well," says the vet, "Let's have a look at him."

So he picks the dog up and examines his eyes, then checks his teeth.

Finally, he says "I'm going to have to put him down."

"What? Because he's cross-eyed?"

"No, because he's really heavy."

C-17

*****

"Everyone was so shocked last week when grandpa died."

"Your grandpa died? How old was he?"

"He was ninety five."

"Ninety five? Why was everyone shocked?"

"Because his parachute didn't open."

C-18

*****

Psychiatry students were in their Emotional Extremes class. "Let's set some parameters," the professor said. "What's the opposite of joy?" he asked one student.

"Sadness," he replied.

"The opposite of depression?" he asked another student.

"Elation," he replied.

"The opposite of woe?" the prof asked a young woman from Texas.

The Texan replied, "Sir, I believe that would be giddyup."

C-19

*****

An old man is lying on his deathbed. The doctors have confirmed that the waiting will be over within the next twenty-four hours. Suddenly the old man opens his eyes.

"I must be dreaming! I smell my favorite cookies baking in the kitchen! My wife must be baking them for me as a final gesture of farewell."

Tears well up in the old man's eyes as he thinks about his wife baking his favorite cookies so that the smell would comfort him in his final hours. He was greatly moved by her courage. Then he got to thinking that if she could be so courageous to bake the cookies at such a difficult time, he would find the courage to get to the kitchen to have one last cookie.

So the old man pulled himself from his bed. He didn't have the strength to stand on his feet, so he began to crawl down the hallway, toward the kitchen. The smell of the freshly baked cookies grew ever stronger, and his determination to have one grew stronger as well.

Finally he reached the kitchen and saw the plate of cookies cooling on the counter. He reached up with a trembling hand to take a cookie, when suddenly his fingers were smacked by a spatula, and his wife snapped at him.

"Don't touch those, they're for the funeral guests!"

C-20

*****

I saw a news report about a dentist who removed a thirty-pound tusk from an elephant.

The hard part was getting the elephant to spit in the little sink.

C-21

*****

A new bride set her dinner table with a proud smile on her face. Her young husband sat down and started to eat.

The bride casually commented: "The best things I cook are meatloaf and peach cobbler."

Her husband politely cleared his throat and asked:

"Which is this?"

C-22

*****

Why does a mermaid wear seashells?

Because "B" shells are too small and "D" shells are too big!

C-23

*****

A guy has a talking dog. He brings it to a talent scout.

"This dog can speak English," He claims to the unimpressed agent.

"Okay, Sport," The guys says to the dog, "What's on the top of a house?"

"Roof!" The dog replies.

"Oh, come on..." the talent agent responds. "All dogs go 'roof'."

"No, wait," the guy says. He asks the dog, "What does sandpaper feel like?"

"Rough!" The dog answers.

The talent agent gives a condescending blank stare. He is losing his patience.

"No, hang on," the guy says. "This one will amaze you." He turns and asks the dog: "Who, in your opinion, was the greatest baseball player of all time?"

"Ruth!" goes the dog. And the talent scout, having seen enough, boots them out of his office onto the street.

And the dog turns to the guy and says, "Maybe I shoulda said DiMaggio?"

C-24

*****

An old Cowboy sat down at the Bar and ordered a Drink. As he sat sipping his Drink, a young pretty young woman sat down next to him.

She turned to the cowboy and asked, "Are you a real Cowboy?"

He replied, "Well, I've spent my whole life, breaking colts, working cows, going to rodeos, fixing fences, pulling calves, bailing hay, doctoring calves, cleaning my barn, fixing flats, working on tractors, and feeding my dogs, so I guess I am a cowboy."

She nodded and said, "Well, I know what you mean. I'm a 'Lesbian'. I spend my whole day thinking about women. As soon as I get up in the morning, I think about women. When I shower, I think about women. When I watch TV, I think about women. I even think about women when I eat. It seems that everything makes me think of women."

The two shook their heads in wonder and sat sipping in silence.

A little while later, a man sat down on the other side of the old Cowboy and asked him, "Are you a real Cowboy?"

He replied, "I always thought I was, but I just found out I'm a 'Lesbian'."

C-25

*****

A young bride and her husband were about to consummate their marriage. The groom gazed into his new wife's eyes and said,

"Darling, am I the first?"

The bride responded,

"Why does everybody keep asking me that?"

C-26

*****

The ship was sinking.

The captain called the passengers and crew together and asked,

“Is there anybody here who can really pray?”

One passenger said,

“I can really pray! I pray all the time!”

The captain said,

“That’s great, because we’re short one life jacket.”

C-27

*****

Two elderly ladies meet at the market after not seeing each other for some time. One asked how the other's husband was doing. “Oh! Rodger died last week. He went out to the garden to dig up a cabbage for dinner, had a heart attack and dropped dead right there in the vegetable patch.”

“Oh dear, I'm sorry,” replied her friend, “What did you do?”

“Opened a can of peas instead.”

C-28

*****

Man calls home.

Maid answers phone.

He says, “Can I speak to my wife?”

She says, “No, she's upstairs in bed with her boyfriend.”

He's mad—says, “Ok, go to the hall closet and take out my shotgun. Go upstairs and kill them both."

Being the loyal maid, she says, "Ok."

Five minutes later she picks up the phone and says, "Ok, they're both dead.

What should I do with the bodies?"

He says, "Throw them in the pool, and I'll take care of them when I get home."

She says, "We don't have a pool."

He asks, "Is this 555-1234?"

C-29

*****

A photographer for a national magazine was assigned to take pictures of a great forest fire. He was advised that a small plane would be waiting to fly him over the fire.

The photographer arrived at the airstrip just an hour before sundown. Sure enough, a small Cessna airplane was waiting. He jumped in with his equipment and shouted, "Let's go!" The tense man sitting in the pilot's seat swung the plane into the wind and soon they were in the air, though flying erratically.

"Fly over the north side of the fire," said the photographer, "And make several low-level passes."

Why?" asked the nervous pilot.

"Because I'm going to take pictures!" yelled the photographer. "I'm a photographer, and photographers take pictures!"

The pilot replied, "You mean you're not the flight instructor?"

C-30

*****

A travelling salesman becomes friendly with Mary, the waitress in a hotel coffee shop, and invites her up to his room. She is offended.

The man says, "Don't get excited! This is all in the Bible!" Mary calms down.

After Mary is finished at work, they go to a café and have some drinks and dances. The man invites Mary up to his room and she gets angry again.

The man explains, "It's in the Bible!"

Soon they are in the man's room. He suggests that they undress and have some fun. He assures Mary that it's in the Bible.

Mary objects again. "Where? Where does it say that? Show me where this all is in the Bible!"

The man takes the Bible from the nightstand drawer and shows the inside cover where someone had written: "For a good time, call Mary the waitress."

C-31

*****

Two guys were discussing popular family trends on sex, marriage, and Family values.

Bill said, 'I didn't sleep with my wife before we got married, did you?'

Larry replied, 'I'm not sure, what was her maiden name?

C-32

*****

On her son's seventeenth birthday, a mother pleadingly asked,

“Son, promise me you won't smoke! Please don't let me find out you've been smoking from idle gossip in the neighborhood.”

“Don't worry about me,” replied her son. “I quit smoking a year ago.”

C-33

*****

His wife had been killed in an accident and the police were questioning the old gentleman.

“Did she say anything before she died?” asked the sergeant.

“She spoke without interruption for about forty years,” he answered.

C-34

*****

Bob frequently attends his church Bingo club, where every week a gag door prize is given out. One week, Bob is presented with a toilet brush.

"What the hell is this?" he asks the pastor.

"Why, it's a toilet brush."

"Ooh, I see," says Bob.

A couple weeks later, the pastor jokingly asks Bob how the brush is working.

"Well, it's okay, but I think I'll go back to using paper."

C-35

*****

"We want to ask you to help identify the body." Said the officer to the young man.

"We're almost sure he's your brother. The identification we found says his name was Reese, but the body is all torn apart."

The young man nodded bravely.

"I'll try to help."

The officer uncovered the body and the young man spoke up.

"Yes, those are Reese's pieces."

C-36

*****

The sergeant growled at the young soldier.

"Jenkins! I didn't see you at camouflage training this morning."

Private Jenkins answered with a salute.

"Thank you very much, Sir!"

C-37

*****

A young man was visiting his wife's family for Sunday dinner. As he sat down at the table, his mother-in-law was already there offering him mashed potatoes.

"One scoop or two?"

"Just one, thank you." Replied the young man.

"It's okay," the mother-in-law prodded, "You don't need to be polite."

"Well then," began the young man nervously, "Just one scoop you ugly, prying old witch."

Chapter Two

About This Book

This book contains jokes to tell, and instructions on how to tell them. I didn't write these jokes, I collected them. There's a difference between the comedy routines that you see on television, and jokes that are told and passed around. Comedians on TV don't tell jokes. Very talented comedians write their own comedy routines. I'm not trying to teach you to do that in this book.

These jokes have been told and shared many times.

One important note here:

This book doesn't contain just any jokes. These aren't regular jokes, or common jokes. These are the best jokes I've been able to collect. These are my favorite jokes. I've put literally years of study and research into finding the best jokes available.

What if you don't agree?

If you don't think the jokes here are funny, then you really need to do some research and study of your own. And you can stick it in your ear. I don't know. I suppose funny is subject to personal taste. You need to discover what is funny to you. But believe me: The jokes in this book are funny. I'm confident that these are the funniest jokes you'll find.

Why am I so confident?

Let's look at my process of study.

When I purchase a book of jokes, or get one from the library, I'm always making notes of the best jokes in the collection. I do the same when I find web pages of jokes on the internet.

So far, nothing unusual in my methods. But one thing interesting always happens when I look over a collection of jokes. I always notice that 90 to 99 percent of the jokes in the collection are absolutely terrible. I mean they're awful, stupid, unusable, a waste of time, and an insult to the dimmest person's intelligence. These jokes should be discarded and forgotten. They lower the standard of all jokes. They aren't even jokes by my standards, they are just stupid collections of words. Clearly these stupid jokes get me worked up. And I find these collections of festering jokes everywhere. They appear in physical books and on websites. So, out of any given collection of jokes that I've ever looked through, I've only ever found a very few good jokes. Sometimes I've looked through a collection of jokes without finding even one good joke.

Now, this is all my opinion, right? Maybe. But I believe that my lifetime experience of seeking out the best jokes has given me some ability to distinguish a good joke from a bad joke. This is the ability I want to help you develop.

This ability to distinguish bad from good is developed in us no matter what the subject. For example, if you listen to any genre of music with enough attention and dedication, you'll learn to distinguish good music from bad. The same is true for movies. If you love, watch and study movies, you'll develop a criteria for knowing which movies are good and which are bad. If you hear, and think about good jokes and bad jokes, you'll start to have favorites, and you'll learn with are good and which are bad.

Most people don't concentrate and study when hearing jokes. They're not thinking about proper elements of humor. They're not judging tempo, or cadence, and they're not checking to see if the facts agree. They're just being entertained. When you're working on learning about jokes and humor, you're going to listen more intently, and you'll really learn to distinguish good jokes from bad ones.

Now, some people can't distinguish good jokes from bad jokes because they have no class. To them, humor means four letter words, or references to poop and other bodily functions. Leave those people to their stupid fate. We'll discuss crude humor later in this book.

What other qualifications do I have as a judge of jokes and humor? Okay. Here goes: I'm a funny guy. I'm not a stand-up comedian. I tried my hand at stand-up comedy, and failed. It's the hardest kind of performance I've ever tried. It's absolutely terrifying. I have the highest degree of respect for stand-up comics that you can imagine. I just couldn't do it.

So my focus here is my experience telling jokes to friends and small groups.

When I've shared stupid jokes, or have delivered them poorly, people have groaned. Every one of those failed jokes was a great lesson to me. When I've told good jokes, people really laugh hard. So I've learned to gage the reactions of an audience.

Input from others. That's what it comes down to. People share jokes with me, and they critique me when I tell jokes. That's the part of learning about joke telling that I cherish the most. People like to hear me tell jokes. I'm always asked to tell a joke when I'm part of any kind of group. People frequently comment on my ability to tell a joke, and even ask me to finish a joke after they've started telling one.

I don't say any of this to boast, but only to demonstrate that I've put a lot of work into developing my taste in jokes, and my ability to tell jokes. The impact on my life has been more than just the development of my sense of humor. I've had to learn to be comfortable speaking in front of others. I've had to learn to control my delivery and my memory. The same can happen for you. Maybe you'll hate some of the jokes in this book. It doesn't matter. Do the same things that I've done, and you'll tell great jokes.

Let's get started with some homework:

I want you to do some observation.

Go find some funny things, situations and people.

Go ask a few people to tell you a joke. If they don't have a joke to tell, have them read one of the jokes in the book to you. Pay attention to how they approach and deliver a joke.

Pay close attention to how he or she tells jokes. If you can, ask them to tell you about their own joke telling method.

Listen to a funny entertainer, like a comedian. They might be on television or on the internet. Make notes about their style, their demeanor, their delivery.

Start collecting jokes. Find lots of sources of jokes, and collect the best ones. Make an effort to archive your jokes so that they can be studied and referenced. This means actually putting them in print, and filing them away. Later, you need to study them regularly so that they will be on the tip of your tongue when they are needed.

Once you've got a good collection of jokes, you need to practice telling them, a subject we will discuss later. For now, this means that you need to regularly "try out" your jokes on people who you know will listen at least politely. Ask them to be critical. Ask them to tell you what they think you're doing right and wrong.

Maybe right now you're a little disappointed. You don't think that joke telling should require work. Maybe you think humor should just flow naturally. Being funny is not like having blonde hair or blue eyes. Being funny is like playing the piano. It takes work and practice. You need to pay attention and practice the things you learn in this book, because there's nothing worse than charity laughs when jokes are bad. And yet, while joke telling is a talent like playing the piano, it's also very different. You can't practice joke telling when you're alone. You can't tell a joke without an audience.

I want you to find a practice audience. Someone, or some small group, who will listen willingly to your jokes, and be on your side. Have them tell you what they liked about your jokes, your style and your delivery. Then have them give you suggestions on how you could improve.

Be ready to learn! If your audience does what they're supposed to do, they'll have criticisms. That will hurt. But you'll learn. And you've got this collection of jokes in this book to use as tools.

I've indexed the jokes in this book very carefully by section. This will aid you as you pick the jokes that are best for your style, and then work hard at practicing. Silly jokes, ridiculous jokes, double meaning jokes, surprise jokes. Learn to know the difference, learn which ones work best for you.

How you react to jokes, and whether or not you "get" a joke is a big part of learning a joke and being able to share it with others. Your reaction even determines whether or not a joke is funny in the moment.

When I was a kid, I took guitar lessons from a wonderful man in my neighborhood. Renny was a great teacher and friend to his guitar students. One day a girl in my guitar class asked Renny if he used to go swimming when he was a child.

She was suddenly in the spotlight.

She was leading up to something.

She was telling a joke.

Renny smiled enthusiastically and replied that indeed he had gone swimming as a child.

"Weren't you afraid that the dinosaurs would bite your toes?"

Everyone in the class roared with laughter except me. I just didn't get it. I sat there and thought and thought. After a good long pause, the punch line cleared up for me.

"Oh! I get it!" I shouted triumphantly.

Renny smiled at me warmly. My delayed response had squashed their joke.

"Thank you, my friend."

Joke Section D: Stupid

Please note: Stupid jokes are meant to be stupid. That's the point. That's why they're funny. When someone hears a stupid joke, and then declares: "that was stupid!" well, it makes them look stupid. It's the same as announcing that they didn't get the joke.

D-1

*****

During a training session at an artillery unit the sergeant-major was busy describing how the sophisticated aiming device of the artillery weapon system is used:

"As you all know, there are 180 degrees in a circle."

One of the soldiers put up his hand and said: "But there are 360 degrees in a circle, sergeant-major."

"You idiot," replied the sergeant-major, "I am obviously speaking about a small circle!"

D-2

*****

This guy is looking to buy a saw to cut down some trees in his backyard. He goes to a chainsaw shop and asks about various chainsaws.

The dealer tells him, "Look, I have a lot of models, but why don't you save yourself a lot of time and aggravation and get the top-of- the-line model. This chainsaw will cut a hundred cords of wood for you in one day."

So, the man takes the chainsaw home and begins working on the trees. After cutting for several hours and only cutting two cords, he decides to quit. He thinks there is something wrong with the chainsaw. "How can I cut for hours and only cut two cords?" the man asks himself. "I will begin first thing in the morning and cut all day," the man tells himself.

So, the next morning the man gets up at 4 am in the morning and cuts and cuts, and cuts till nightfall, and still he only manages to cut five cords.

The man is convinced this is a bad saw. "The dealer told me it would cut one hundred cords of wood in a day, no problem. I will take this saw back to the dealer," the man says to himself.

The very next day the man brings the saw back to the dealer and explains the problem. The dealer, baffled by the man's claim, removes the chainsaw from the case. The dealer says, "Hmm, it looks fine."

Then the dealer starts the chainsaw, to which the man responds, "What's that noise?

D-3

*****

A cop pulls over a blonde for speeding. The cop gets out of his car and asks the blonde for her license.

'You cops should get it together. One day you take away my license, and the next day you ask me to show it."

This joke must showcase the girl's confusion and not our view of her as stupid.

D-4

*****

A guy's wife gets a new cell phone from her husband.

The next day she goes to Wal-mart and her phone rings, so she answers it.

It was her husband. He says, "How's the new cell phone?"

She replied, "Great...but how did you know I was at Wal-mart?"

D-5

*****

I bought a new necktie. I really liked the colors and the design but I had to take it back. The clerk asked me what was wrong with it and I told him. "It's too tight!"

D-6

*****

Two guys were driving a semi down a country highway when they came to a viaduct. The sign said 10 feet zero inches, so they stopped to measure their truck. Unfortunately, the truck was just over 12 feet high.

"We can't go on, the sign says 10 feet, and we're more than 12 feet high."

The other guy carefully looked both directions down the highway.

"I don't see any cops, let's go for it!"

D-7

*****

A man had two horses, but he couldn't tell them apart. So he asked his neighbor for advice. He suggested that she cut the tail off one of the horses. This worked until the other horse snagged his tail on a fence. So the neighbor suggested notching one of the horses' ear. This worked until the other horse snagged his ear on a fence. So the neighbor suggested measuring the heights of the horses. And sure enough, the white horse was two inches taller than the black horse.

D-8

*****

A man at work grabs his lunch sack when the lunch bell rings. Opening his bag at the lunch table, he groans.

"Oh crap! Tuna!"

The next day he gathers in the lunch room with his co-workers again and opens his lunch.

"Dang! Tuna again!"

The next day he's at the table again with his lunch bag.

"Dangit! Tuna again!"

His co-workers ask him:

"Why don't you ask your wife to make something other than Tuna for your lunch?"

"Oh, that would never work." Replied the man.

"Why not?" asked his friends.

"I make my own lunches."

D-9

*****

A young guy got a job as a trainee in a supermarket.

On his first day at work, he arrived early, eager to make a good impression. The manager welcomed him with a warm smile and giving him a broom, said, "Your first job will be to sweep the floor."

The young guy protested, "But I'm a college graduate!"

"Oh, I'm so sorry. I didn't realize that" said the manager. "Here, hand me the broom, I will show you how to sweep the floor."

D-10

*****

Two country brothers are traveling to the big city to attend college. Before they leave home, their dad gives them both a bit of advice:

"You watch them big city cab drivers. They'll rob you blind. Don't you go paying them what they ask. You haggle."

At the airport, the brothers catch a cab to their hotel. When they reach their destination, the cabbie says, "That'll be twenty dollars, boys."

"Oh no you don't! My dad warned me about you. You'll only be getting fifteen dollars from me," says one of the boys.

"And you'll only be getting fifteen from me too," adds the other.

D-11

*****

The new boss was determined to rid the company of all slackers. On a tour of the facilities, the CEO noticed a guy leaning against a wall. The room was full of workers and he wanted to let them know that he meant business. He asked the guy,

"How much money do you make a week?"

A little surprised, the young man looked at him and said, "I make $400 a week. Why?"

The CEO said, "Wait right here."

He walked back to his office, came back in two minutes, and handed the guy $1,600 in cash and said, "Here's four weeks' pay. Now GET OUT and don't come back."

Feeling pretty good about himself the CEO looked around the room and asked, "Does anyone want to tell me what that goof-ball did here?"

From across the room a voice said, "He's the pizza delivery guy from Domino's."

D-12

*****

Two elderly ladies had been friends for many decades. Over the years, they had shared all kinds of activities and adventures. Lately, their activities had been limited to meeting a few times a week to play cards.

One day, they were playing cards when one looked at the other and said,

"Now don't get mad at me. I know we've been friends for a long time, but I just can't think of your name! I've thought and thought, but I can't remember it. Please tell me what your name is."

Her friend glared at her.

For at least three minutes she just stared and glared at her. Finally

she said, "How soon do you need to know?"

D-13

*****

As this man was driving down the freeway, his cell phone rang.

Answering, he heard his wife's voice urgently warning him,

"Herman, I just heard on the news that there's a car going the wrong way the freeway. Please be careful!"

"It's not just one car," said Herman, "It's hundreds of them!"

D-14

*****

So these two politicians come out and discover they've locked their keys in the car. The first one says "I guess we'll have to do the old coat hanger trick <sigh>"

"Do you know **how** to do the coat hanger trick" asks the second?

"Well, we could crawl in through the open window" offers the first.

"But if we do that" the second objects "People will think we're too stupid to do the coat hanger trick."

"Well we'd better do something!" says the first "because it looks like rain and the top's down!"

D-15

*****

A blonde canvassed a wealthy neighborhood looking for odd jobs. She went to the front door of the first house and asked the owner if he had anything for her to do.

"Well, you can paint my porch. How much will you charge?"

"How about $50?"

The man agreed and told her the paint was in the garage. A short time later, the blonde came to the door to collect her money.

"You're finished already?" he asked.

"Yes," the blonde answered, "and I had paint left over, so I gave it two coats." Impressed, the man reached in his pocket for the $50.

"And by the way," the blonde added, "that's not a Porch, it's a Ferrari."

D-16

*****

Judi stormed up to the front desk of the library and said, "I have a complaint!"

"Yes, ma'am?"

"I borrowed a book last week and it was horrible!"

"What was wrong with it?"

"It had way too many characters and there was no plot whatsoever!"

The librarian nodded and said, "Ah. So you must be the person who took our phone book."

D-17

*****

George's father really wanted him to play on the high school football team. He went to see the coach to plead his case.

"Coach, I just know my boy George would make a good player on your team! I just know it!"

The coach looked at George's father and rubbed his chin.

"Well, for George to play on my team, he's going to need three things. First, he'll need dedication."

George's father looked the coach right in the eye.

"Coach, George has got plenty of dedication!"

The coach continued.

"Second, he'll need stamina."

George's father jumped to his feet.

"Coach, George has got all kinds of stamina!"

The coach nodded his head.

"And third, he'll need intelligence."

"Uh, he's got his own football shoes."

D-18

*****

Paddy wanted to be an accountant, so he went for an aptitude test.

Tester: If I give you two rabbits, two rabbits, and another two rabbits, how many rabbits have you got?

Paddy: Seven!

Tester: No, listen carefully again.

If I give you two rabbits, two rabbits, and another two rabbits, how many rabbits have you got?

Paddy: Seven! Tester: Let's try this another way.

If I give you two bottles of beer, two bottles of beer, and another two bottles of beer, how many bottles of beer have you got?

Paddy: Six. Tester: Good"

Now, if I give you two rabbits, two rabbits, and another two rabbits, how many rabbits have you got?

Paddy: Seven! Tester: How on earth do you work out that three lots of two rabbits is seven?

Paddy: I've already got one rabbit at home!

D-19

*****

A crook mistakenly made a counterfeit $8 bill instead of a $10 bill. He decided to try it out anyway.

He went to the teller at the local bank and asked for change.

The teller looked at the $8 bill and gave the crook two $4 bills as change.

D-20

*****

A life-long city man, tired of the rat race, decided he was going to give up the city life, move to the country, and become a chicken farmer. He bought a nice, used chicken farm and moved in. As it turned out, his next door neighbor was also a chicken farmer. The neighbor came for a visit one day and said, "Chicken farming isn't easy. Tell you what. To help you get started, I'll give you 100 chickens."

The new chicken farmer was thrilled. Two weeks later the neighbor dropped by to see how things were going. The new farmer said,

"Not too well. All 100 chickens died."

The neighbor said, "Oh, I can't believe that. I've never had any trouble with my chickens. I'll give you 100 more."

Another two weeks went by and the neighbor stopped by again. The new farmer said, "You're not going to believe this, but the second 100 chickens died too." Astounded, the neighbor asked, "What went wrong?"

The new farmer said, "Well, I'm not sure whether I'm planting them too deep or too close together."

Tell this joke as if you were very unsure and give the punch line as if you were very confused.

D-21

*****

Bill gets called into the manager's office. The boss asks him to sit down.

"Bill," he says, "We both know you're not the brightest spark here, but over the past five years you've never been late or sick even one time, and I think you deserve a reward. So, how does a new car sound?"

Bill shrugged his shoulders and said, "Vrooom! Vrooooom!"

D-22

*****

A lady and her husband are lying in bed listening to the next door neighbor's dog.

It has been in the backyard barking for hours & hours.

The lady jumps up out of bed and says,

"I've had enough of this!"

She goes downstairs.

The lady finally comes back up to bed and her husband says,

"The dog is still barking, what have you been doing?"

The lady says,

"I put the dog in our backyard, let's see how THEY like it!"

D-23

*****

Two girls are living together while attending college. The first came home from work one day and the other had a rope around her waist. The first asked the second why she had a rope tied around her waist. The second answered that she was trying to commit suicide.

The first said, "You're supposed to put the rope around your neck."

The second replied, "I tried that but I couldn't breathe!"

D-24

*****

Two hippies are standing on opposite sides of each other on a riverbank. One hippie yells to the other, "Duuuude! How do I get to the other side?"

The other hippie thinks a second and yells back, "DUUUUDE! You're ON the other side!"

D-25

*****

A man learning to fly a helicopter jumps in and takes off. Goes up to 800 feet. Suddenly, down he comes and crashes!

"What happened?" asked the flight controller.

"It got chilly up there, so I turned off the fan!"

D-26

*****

I ordered a foot-long sandwich from a take-out restaurant and asked the clerk to cut it into fourths.

"I'm sorry, I can't," she said. "I already cut it in half."

This joke could actually happen to any of us in a sandwich shop. It's an example of a truth turned into a joke.

D-27

*****

A church lady was driving down the street in a sweat because she had an important meeting and couldn't find a parking space. Looking up toward heaven, she said,

"Lord, take pity on me. If you find me a parking place I'll go to Mass every Sunday for the rest of my life and give up drinking wine."

Miraculously, a parking space opened up right in front of her destination.

The woman looked up to heaven and said,

"Never mind, Lord; I found one on my own."

D-28

*****

A funeral service is held for a woman who just passed away. As the pallbearers carry the casket out, they accidentally bump into a wall. They hear a faint moan. They open the casket and find that the woman is actually alive.

She lives for 10 more years and then dies. They have another funeral for her. At the end of the service, the pallbearers carry out the casket.

As they are walking, the husband cries out, "Watch out for the wall!"

D-29

*****

A young man from the city went to visit his farmer uncle. For the first few days, the uncle showed him the usual things - chickens, cows, crops, etc. After three days, however, it was obvious that the nephew was getting bored, and the uncle was running out of things to amuse him with.

Finally, the uncle decided to give them a real treat. “Why don't you grab a gun, take my prized hunting dogs, and go have some fun shooting?”

This seemed to cheer the nephew up, and with enthusiasm, off he went, dogs in trail.

After a few hours, the nephew returned.

“How did you enjoy that?” asked the uncle.

“It was great!” exclaimed the nephew. “Got any more dogs?”

D-30

*****

A kid from the football team was bragging about his knowledge of the state capitals.

He proudly said, “Go ahead, ask me, I know all of them.”

The teacher said, “OK, what's the capital of Wisconsin?”

The kid replied, “That's easy - 'W'.”

D-31

*****

What happened?” asked the hospital visitor of the heavily bandaged man sitting up in bed.

“Well, I went down to the amusement park this weekend and decided to take a ride on the roller coaster. As we came up to the top of the highest loop, I noticed a little sign by the side of the track.

“I tried to read it but it was very small and I couldn't make it out. I was so curious that I decided to ride the coaster again, but we went by so quickly that I couldn't see what the sign said.

"By now, I was determined to read that sign so I went 'round a third time. As we reached the top, I stood up in the car to get a better view."

"And did you manage to see what the sign said this time?" asked the visitor.

"Yes."

"What did it say?"

"Don't stand up in the car!"

D-32

*****

Two elderly women were out driving in a large car, both could barely see over the dashboard. As they were cruising along, they came to an intersection. The stoplight was red, but they just went on through.

The woman in the passenger seat thought to herself "I must be losing it. I could have sworn we just went through a red light."

After a few more minutes, they came to another intersection and the light was red again.

Again, they went right through. The woman in the passenger seat was almost sure that the light had been red but was really concerned that she was losing it.

She was getting nervous. At the next intersection, sure enough, the light was red and they went on through. So, she turned to the other woman and said,

"Mildred, do you know that we just ran through three red lights in a row? You could have killed us both!"

Mildred turned to her and said, "Oh, am I driving?"

D-33

*****

Bubba tells his friends all about his new Thermos Jug. "It keeps hot things hot and cold things cold".

"So what do you have in there?" They want to know.

"Hot stew and iced tea."

D-34

*****

A man's father dies, and he visits with the undertaker.

"I want the best for my father, only the best! He was a wonderful man and I want the classiest, best burial that money can buy!"

The undertaker agrees, and the father is buried.

A month goes by and the man receives a bill from the undertaker for $16,085.

He gladly pays the bill.

Another month passes and the man receives a bill from the undertaker for $85.

He pays the bill without question.

Another month passes and another bill arrives in the amount of $85.

Then another month passes with another bill for $85.

The man visits the undertaker again.

"I appreciate the care you took in burying my father, but I just have to ask you why I continue to receive a bill for $85.00 each month."

The undertaker explains:

"You said you wanted your father's burial to be first-class, so I rented a Tuxedo for him."

D-35

*****

A man who owned a donkey would lead the donkey each night to its stall. But the stall doorway was too short, and the donkey's ears would brush the top of the doorway, causing the donkey to kick violently.

The man decided to fix this problem one day and got his hand saw out and started working on the top of the doorway.

The man's neighbor had stopped by and was watching him work.

"Wouldn't it be easier to dig out the floor at the entrance to the stall to give the donkey more space to get through?"

The donkey's own spun around angrily.

"Idiot!" he fumed. "His ears are too long, not his legs!"

CHAPTER THREE

YOU'RE A PERFORMER

If you're going to tell a joke, then you have an audience, and you're a performer, whether you like it or not. You're going to tell a joke, and someone's going to look at you and listen to your joke. Jokes are not for the shy, or those who don't want to get noticed. If you're going to tell a joke, we have to assume that you want to be the center of attention, even if it's just for a moment.

You need to know that audiences are cruel and hostile by their very nature.

What?

They all seem like such nice people.

But think about it. An audience is daring you to entertain them. And if, at any moment, they don't feel entertained, they will let you know about it, one way or another.

This is especially true when you tell a joke. Yes, your audience will enjoy a laugh if your joke works, but often they would enjoy your joke MORE if it doesn't. They want you to fail. They want your joke to bomb. That would be as funny, if not MORE funny than if your joke worked. They think you are arrogant for daring to tell a joke. This is why you need to follow the program laid out in this book. For example: don't announce your joke, or ask permission to tell a joke. If your audience is prepared, they'll rout against you. Surprise will help your joke succeed.

Sometimes you find your jokes first, and then later find your audience. Your audience might be one person you stopped in the hallway, or fifty people sitting at tables listening to your show.

Sometimes, you'll find your audience first, and then you must scramble to find your jokes. Again, here is a situation that requires some preparation. If you have an arsenal of jokes, and you've had some experience telling them, you'll be ready.

Your new found audience might be one person who likes a good laugh, or it might be a business meeting of professionals that are waiting for you to give a presentation. You audience might be people sitting in a lunchroom with you, or riding a bus.

Some audiences, or some people in your audiences will not like jokes. They don't think jokes are dignified, or at least that's what they say. The truth is probably that they don't get jokes. I believe that what these people REALLY don't like is the feeling of being left out.

If people have been hurt or embarrassed by a joke sometime in the past, they won't be very receptive to your attempts to tell a joke. How you deal with sharing jokes with these people is very important.

As a joke-teller, you're performing valuable public service. People need cheering up. Funny people do their work even when they're not in the mood. But be very careful! Understand that there will be times when shrugging your shoulders and deciding to keep your joke for another occasion will be the right thing to do.

But even if you do find the right moment to share a joke, there are some things you need to remember about people who have paused to hear your joke. They expect you to be funny, but they expect you to know when it's enough.

You'll do better if you have two or more jokes to tell.

Why?

People get defensive when they hear one joke. They're likely to resist laughing. They'll tell you your joke is bad, or silly, or stupid.

But now they're primed.

The second joke will always make them chuckle.

If you can tell a third and a fourth joke, you'll own your audience. You'll have them gasping for breath. They'll be laughing so hard that they will hardly be able to hold themselves up.

Is this because your jokes are so funny?

No, it's not that.

People like to laugh. They want to laugh.

They just need you to flirt with them. They want to be tickled a little bit first.

So, no, people don't laugh at your jokes because they're so amazingly funny. And they don't laugh because you're such an amazing performer.

But it doesn't hurt if you have some good jokes to tell, and some proper instruction for correct joke telling.

There is skill in this. You need to know your jokes, and you need to know how to tickle your audience, and you need to know how to effectively deliver your jokes.

So, back to what we said first

Don't overdo it. Don't be the life of the party. Tell a joke, and then wait to see if another would be appropriate. If you start telling jokes, and then don't stop, your audience will turn hostile.

Don't interrupt. Please don't interrupt. No one's dying to hear your joke. Don't be dying to tell it.

Don't expect to be begged. That's a tough one. You've got a joke to tell, and maybe you're waiting for an invitation to tell it. That invitation will never come. You're going to find the right moment to insert your joke into a conversation.

There are other roles you play, apart from performer. You're a salesman. You have to create the mood. You have to convince your audience that they want to laugh, that they want to be entertained. You're not going to ask permission, or announce your intentions, but you're going to signal your audience in some way that you're taking the floor, and you're going to entertain them.

Yes, you're a performer, and performers aren't shy. Unless being shy is part of your routine.

So here's your basic instruction set for telling a joke:

Relax, jokes are for the easy going. Don't be anxious. Be easy going. Jokes are not serious business.

Wait, the right opportunity to tell your joke is coming.

Now, this is very important. You need to make sure you have your audience's attention. You need to be assertive. If you're audience starts to pay attention to what you're saying halfway through your joke, they won't get it. Speak with authority and look people in the eye. Speak with a steady, strong pace, so that people won't interrupt you.

If you're going to tell a joke, your joke should be entertaining. You're not sharing a recipe for brownies, you're not informing people what kind of gas mileage they should expect from their car.

Be ready to perform. Don't clear your throat while you're telling your joke. If you're eating a twinkie, finish eating your twinkie before you tell your joke. We don't want to hear annoying bodily sounds. And don't blow kisses at me! I don't want to hear you smack your lips at me.

Be ready. Know your joke, and don't get confused.

So what kind of performing demeanor should you adopt?

In the telling of your joke, sometimes you'll sound very serious, sometimes you'll sound silly, or crazy.

But your overall demeanor as a performer should be smug. Yes, I said smug. You're a little imp. You little devil you! You're telling a joke. You think you're funny. But be careful, I don't want you to announce your joke and I don't want you to hijack the occasion, or demand to be the center of attention.

But gosh dang it, you think you're funny. Be smug.

Just don't be smug for a long time. Be smug while telling your joke, and for a short time afterward. Then drop it and just try to be pleasant.

But hang on a minute, isn't smugness an undesirable quality?

Sure it is, but it's needed for joke telling.

Observe comedians and humorous actors on tv. They're smug. And there's a reason. There is nothing more important to the success of a joke, than the confidence the teller has in telling the joke.

There is also an indescribable element to success in joke telling. There is no magic joke, there is no magic answer that will help you be funnier and more humorous. It's all work, practice, and an illusion that you create.

Funny people tickle their audience a little. They flirt. They convince their audience to giggle with them, just a little bit. Then step by step, they lead them to big laughs and hardy hars.

Yes, the technique must be developed, and the joke teller much put in the work to get the jokes right. But we're laughing with the performer because he sold us on the idea that it would be fun to laugh along.

Should you laugh at your own jokes? Maybe. Sometimes. But at least wait for your audience to laugh first.

As you read this book, you'll find specific instructions on how to tell specific jokes. I encourage you to follow these instructions carefully. But keep in mind that by practicing and developing joke telling skills, you'll be developing your own style of joke telling.

You're a performer, and no one tells a joke quite the way you do. I know that's true, and I would never presume to tell you that your own unique style is wrong. I'm just trying to help you avoid bad habits.

Joke Section E: Misdirection

These jokes are a lot of fun. They lead you one way, and the swerve in another direction. It's as if they were saying, "Look, over here, Look! Don't look in my other hand! Awwww, You should have looked in my other hand."

E-1

*****

A golfer is about to tee off, and a greasy little guy runs up to him, and yells, "Wait! Before you tee off, I have something really amazing to show you!"

The golfer, annoyed, says, "What is it?"

"It's a special golf ball," says the guy. "You can never lose it!"

"Whattaya mean," scoffs the golfer, "you can never lose it? What if you hit it into the water?"

"No problem," says the guy. "It floats, and it detects where the shore is, and spins towards it."

"Well, what if you hit it into the woods?"

"Easy," says the guy. "It emits a beeping sound, and you can find it with your eyes closed."

"Okay," says the golfer, impressed. "But what if your round goes late and it gets dark?"

"No problem, sir, this golf ball glows in the dark! I'm telling you, you can never lose this golf ball!"

The golfer buys it at once. "Just one question," he says to the guy. "Where did you get it?"

"I found it."

E-2

*****

A man is driving his five year old to a friend's house when another car races in front and cuts them off, nearly causing an accident.

"Douchebag!" the father yells.

A moment later he realizes the indiscretion, pulls over, and turns to face his son.

"Your father just said a bad word," he says. "I was angry at that driver, but that was no excuse for what I said. It was wrong. But just because I said it, it doesn't make it right, and I don't ever want to hear you saying it. Is that clear?"

His son looks at him and says: "Too late, douchebag."

E-3

*****

This 85-year-old couple, having been married almost 60 years, dies tragically in a car crash. They have been in good health the last ten years, mainly due to the wife's nearly neurotic interest in health food.

When they reached the pearly gates, St. Peter took them to their mansion, which was decked out with a beautiful kitchen and master bath suite, complete with Jacuzzi. As they "oohed and aahed' the old man asked St. Peter how much all this was going to cost.

"It's free," St. Peter replied, "Remember, this is Heaven."

Next they went out back to see the championship golf course the home backed up to. They would have golfing privileges every day, and each week the course changed to a new one representing the great golf courses on Earth.

The old man asked, "What are the green fees?"

"This is Heaven," St. Peter replied. "You play for free."

Next they went to the clubhouse and saw the lavish buffet lunch with the cuisines of the world laid out.

"How much to eat?" asked the old man.

"Don't you understand yet?" St. Peter asked. "This is Heaven. It's free!"

"Well, where are the low-fat and low-cholesterol foods?" the old man asked timidly.

"That's the best part ... you can eat as much as you like of whatever you like and never get fat and you never get sick. This is Heaven."

The old man looked at his wife and said,

"You and your damn bran muffins. I could have been here ten years ago!"

E-4

*****

A woman's husband got a little carried away and began to flirt with the gorgeous blonde playing the piano at the party. But in the course of his exploits he bumped the piano cover and it fell on his hands, so the couple had to leave early.

"Remind me to put a cold pack on your black eye when we get home," said the wife.

"But I haven't got a black eye," he corrected.

"You're not home yet," she reminded.

E-5

*****

A guy asks a lawyer what his fee is.

"I charge $50 for three questions," the lawyer says.

"That's awfully steep, isn't it?" the guy asks.

"Yes," the lawyer replies, "Now what's your final question?"

E-6

*****

The owner of a drug store walks in to find a guy leaning heavily against a wall. The owner asks the clerk, “What’s with that guy over there by the wall?”

The clerk says, “Well, he came in here this morning to get something for his cough. I couldn’t find the cough syrup, so I gave him an entire bottle of laxative.”

The owner says, “You idiot! You can’t treat a cough with laxatives!”

The clerk says, “Oh yeah? Look at him, he’s afraid to cough!”

E-7

*****

A lawyer dies and goes to Heaven. “There must be some mistake,” the lawyer argues. “I’m too young to die. I’m only fifty-five.”

“Fifty-five?” Says Saint Peter. “No, according to our calculations, you’re eighty-two.”

“How’s you get that?” the lawyer asks. Answers St. Peter: “We added up your time sheets.”

E-8

*****

I was yelling at my kid the other day and he replied: “sticks and stones may break my bones but words will never hurt me.” So I threw a dictionary at him.

E-9

*****

The first woman was elected U.S. president. She called her mom to make sure she was coming to the inauguration.

"I don't know, dear. What would I wear?"

"Don't worry, Mom. I've been elected President of the U.S.! I'll send a designer to help you."

"But you know I need special foods for my diet."

"Mom, I'm going to the president. I can get you the food you need."

"But how will I get there?"

"I'll send a Presidential Limo, Mom. Just come!"

"OK, OK, if it makes you happy."

The great day came, and Mama was seated with the future cabinet members. She nudged the man on her right. "See that girl, the one with her hand on the Bible? Her brother's a doctor!"

E-10

*****

Two friends were chatting over lunch.

"I don't know how my folks ever stayed together. They had terrible habits. My dad used to chew and spit and chew and spit and chew and spit."

"Tobacco?" asked the understanding friend.

"No, mom was a terrible cook."

E-11

*****

An 80-year-old lady was marrying for the 4th time. The newspaper sent a reporter to cover the story. The reporter asked if she would mind talking about her first 3 husbands. He wanted to know a little bit about them, like what they did for a living.

The old lady smiled and said "My first husband was a Banker. Then I married a Circus Ringmaster. Next was a Preacher and now in my 80's, a Funeral Director."

When the reporter asked why the four men had such diverse careers. She explained

"I married one for the money, 2 for the show, 3 to get ready & 4 to go......

E-12

*****

Two ladies were visiting over lunch.

One said to the other: "How do you keep your husband from staying out late?"

"Well," said the second lady, "The last time my husband stayed out late, I called to him when he got home. I called, 'Is that you, Jack?"

"How did that help?"

"My husband's name is Robert."

E-13

*****

Last night I ordered a whole meal in French. Even the waiter was amazed –

It was a Chinese restaurant!

E-14

*****

A cowboy rode into town and stopped at the saloon for a drink. Unfortunately, the locals always had a habit of picking on newcomers. When he finished, he found his horse had been stolen.

He comes back into the bar, handily flips his gun into the air, catches it above his head without even looking and fires a shot into the ceiling. “Who stole my horse?” he yelled with surprising forcefulness.

No one answered.

“I'm gonna have another beer and if my horse ain't back outside by the time I'm finished, I'm gonna do what I dun back in Texas and I don't want to have to do what I dun back in Texas!”

Some of the locals shifted restlessly.

He had another beer, walked outside, and his horse was back! He saddled up and started to ride out of town.

The bartender wandered out of the bar and asked, “Say partner, what happened in Texas?”

The cowboy turned back and said, “I had to walk home!”

E-15

*****

Two women are new arrivals at the pearly gates and are comparing stories on how they died:

1st woman: I froze to death.

2nd woman: How horrible.

1st woman: It wasn't so bad. After I quit shaking from the cold, I began to get warm and sleepy, and finally died a peaceful death. What about you?

2nd woman: I died of a massive heart attack. I suspected that my husband was cheating, so I came home early to catch him in the act. But instead, I found him all by himself in the den watching TV.

1st woman: So what happened?

2nd woman: I was so sure there was another woman there somewhere that I started running all over the house looking. I ran up into the attic and searched, and down into the basement. Then I went through every closet and checked under all the beds. I kept this up until I had looked everywhere, and finally I became so exhausted that I just keeled over with a heart attack and died.

1st woman: Too bad you didn't look in the freezer! — We'd both still be alive.

E-16

*****

"Mr. Clark, I've reviewed this case very carefully," the divorce-court judge says, "and I've decided to award your wife $775 a week."

"That's very fair, Your Honor" the husband says. "And every now and then, I'll try to send a few bucks myself."

E-17

*****

Two guys are walking down the street when a mugger approaches them and demands their money. They both grudgingly pull out their wallets and begin taking out their cash.

Just then one guy turns to the other and hands him a bill.

"Here's that $20 I owe you," he says

E-18

*****

Some employees bought their boss a gift for his birthday. Before opening the gift, the boss shook it slightly, and noticed that it was wet in the corner. Touching his finger to the wet spot and tasting it, he asked, "A bottle of wine?"

His employees replied, "No."

Again, he touched his finger to the box and tasted the liquid. "A bottle of scotch?"

"His employees replied again, "No."

Finally the boss asked, "I give up. What is it?"

His workers responded, "A puppy."

E-19

*****

A Spanish captain was walking on his ship when a soldier rushes to him and exclaims, "An enemy ship is approaching us!"

The captain replies calmly, "Go get my red shirt."

The soldier gets the shirt for the captain. The enemy ship comes in and heavy rounds of fire are exchanged. Finally, the Spaniards win.

The soldier asks, "Congrats sir, but why the red shirt?"

The captain replies, "If I got injured, my blood shouldn't be seen, as I didn't want my men to lose hope."

Just then, another soldier runs up and says, "Sir, we just spotted another twenty enemy ships!" The captain calmly replies, "Go bring my yellow pants."

E-20

*****

On the first day of college, the dean addressed the students, pointing out some of the rules: "The female dormitory will be out-of-bounds for all male students, and the male dormitory will be off limits to the female students. Anybody caught breaking this rule will be fined $20 the first time. Anybody caught breaking this rule the second time will be fined $60. Being caught a third time will cost you $180. Are there any questions?"

One student raised his hand and asked, "How much for a season pass?"

E-21

*****

A husband and wife were golfing when suddenly the wife asked,

"Honey, if I died would you get married again?"

The husband said, "No sweetie."

The woman said, "I'm sure you would."

So the man said, "Okay, I would."

Then the woman asked, "Would you let her sleep in our bed?"

And the man replied, "Ya, I guess so."

Then the wife asked, "Would you let her use my golf clubs?"

And the husband replied, "No, she's left-handed."

E-22

*****

A young boy enters a barber shop and the barber whispers to his customer, "This is the dumbest kid in the world. Watch while I prove it to you."

The barber puts a dollar bill in one hand and two quarters in the other, then calls the boy over and asks, "Which do you want, son?"

The boy takes the quarters and leaves.

"What did I tell you?" said the barber. "That kid never learns!"

Later, when the customer leaves, he sees the same young boy coming out of the ice cream store.

"Hey, son! May I ask you a question? Why did you take the quarters instead of the dollar bill?"

The boy licked his cone and replied, "Because the day I take the dollar, the game is over!"

E-23

*****

A bank robber pulls out gun points it at the teller, and says, "Give me all the money or you're geography!"

The puzzled teller replies, "Did you mean to say, "you're history?"

The robber says, "Don't change the subject!"

E-24

*****

A man comes staggering into his house about two o'clock in the morning. His wife waves her fists at him and says,

"If you don't stop this kind of behavior, I'll kill myself!"

The man sneers and says,

"Promises! All I get are promises!"

E-25

*****

A strange old couple from the hills walked into a large department store and asked to see the president.

"How much for your store?"

The president laughed.

"You want to buy this store? Alright. The price to buy this store is 45 million dollars. Have you got 45 million dollars?"

The man said to his wife,

"Gimme that bag you got from under the bed."

The wife handed the man a brown paper bag, and he dumped the contents onto the president's desk. He started counting bundles of bills. The total came to 41 million. The old man groaned and turned to his wife.

"Dammit woman, you brought the wrong bag!"

E-26

*****

A circus owner walked into a bar to see everyone crowded around a table watching a little show. On the table was an upside-down pot and a duck tap dancing on it. The circus owner was so impressed that he offered to buy the duck from its owner.

After some wheeling and dealing, they settled for $10,000 for the duck and the pot.

Three days later the circus owner runs back to the bar in anger,

"Your duck is a rip-off! I put him on the pot before a whole audience and he didn't dance a single step!"

"So?" Asked the duck's former owner, "did you remember to light the candle under the pot?"

E-27

*****

One day this Preacher decided that he would skip church and go hunting.

When in the woods he came upon a bear. He started running, and he ran for a while until all of a sudden he tripped over a tree root. At this moment he was almost face to face with the bear. He dropped to his knees and said, "Dear Lord, if there is one wish I would want for you to give me it would be to make this bear a Christian."

And at that instant…the bear halted to a stop and dropped to his knees and said, "Dear Lord, thank you for the food I am about to receive!"

E-28

*****

A man saw an elderly couple sitting down to lunch at a fast-food restaurant. He noticed that they had ordered just one meal, and as he watched, the older gentleman carefully divided the hamburger in half, then counted out the fries until each had half of them. The old man then began to eat, and his wife sat watching, with her hands folded in her lap.

The young man decided to ask if they would let him buy another meal for them so that they didn't have to split theirs.

The old gentleman said, "Oh, no. We've been married 50 years, and everything has always been and will always be shared 50-50."

The young man asked the wife if she was going to eat, to which she replied, "Not yet. It's his turn to use our teeth."

E-29

*****

A week after John bought a bull, he complained to his friend, “All that bull does is eat grass. Won’t even look at a cow.”

“Take him to the vet,” his friend suggested.

The next week, John is much happier. “The vet gave him some pills, and the bull serviced all of my cows!” he told his pal. “Then he broke through the fence and bred with all my neighbor’s cows! He’s like a machine!”

“What kind of pills were they?” asked the friend.

“I don’t know, but they’ve got a peppermint taste.”

E-30

*****

Feeling edgy, a man took a hot bath.

Just as he became comfortable, the doorbell rang. The man got out of the tub, put on his slippers and robe and went to the door.

A salesman at the door wanted to know if he needed any brushes. Slamming the door, the man returned to the bath.

The doorbell rang again. On went the slippers and robe, and the man started for the door again. He took one step, slipped on a wet spot, fell backward, and hit his back against the hard porcelain bathtub.

Cursing under his breath, the man struggled into his street clothes and with every move a stab of pain, drove to the doctor.

After examining him, the doctor said, “You know, you've been lucky. Nothing is broken. But you need to relax… Why don't you go home and take a long hot bath?”

E-31

*****

An older man goes on a job interview…

Human Resources Manager: “What is your greatest weakness?”

Old Man : “Honesty.”

Human Resources Manager: “I don't think honesty is a weakness.”

Old Man : “I don't really give a damn what you think.”

E-32

*****

The drunk staggered up to the hotel reception and demanded his room be changed.

“But sir,” said the clerk, “you have the best room in the hotel.”

“I insist on another room!!” said the drunk.

“Very good, sir. I`ll change you from 502 to 555. Would you mind telling me why you don't like 502?” asked the clerk.

“Well, for one thing,” said the drunk, “it's on fire.”

E-33

*****

The reverend says to Brother Brown, “Brother Brown, if you had two mansions, would you give one to the Lord?”

Reverend, you know I would give one mansion to the Lord if I had two.”

“And Brother Brown, if you had two Cadillacs, would you give one to the Lord.”

Reverend, you know I would give the Lord a Cadillac if I had two.”

"And Brother Brown, if you had two lawn mowers, would you give one to the Lord?"

"Now hang on a minute there Reverend, you know I have two lawn mowers!"

E-34

*****

A new recruit is standing in formation while the Drill Sargent torments the men.

"You're dreaming of the day when I die, so you can go urinate on my grave, aren't you Private?"

The recruit lifts his chin higher.

"Sir, no sir! After I leave the Army, I'm never going to stand in a line again."

E-35

*****

I just found the worst page in the dictionary. What I saw there was

Disgraceful, disgusting, dishonest, and disingenuous.

E-36

*****

A lady had a streak of gray in her hair. A stranger approached her in a store and said:

"I love your hair! Where did you have that done?"

"Oh thanks!" Replied the lady. "It's natural."

The stranger shook her head with a grimace.

"Oh dear! What are you going to do about it?"

E-37

*****

A man walked into a home improvement store and found a sales clerk.

"I need a chimney. How much does a chimney cost?"

The clerk shrugged.

"Oh, they're on the house."

Chapter Four

Throw it away

Humor is always a contradiction. We belittle important things, and we make a big deal out of trivial things. Never act like your jokes or your joke telling is a big deal. It's just something you're going to throw out there. You're going to quickly drop your contribution to the day on the table and let your audience take it for what it's worth. It's not a big deal! In fact, minimalizing your jokes is going to be your strategy!

Jokes are better when they're thrown away. What does that mean? Jokes are surprises. When you over-sell them, by telling your audience that the following joke is SO FUNNY, you have a lot to live up to. But when you tell a joke with no warning, and tell it with an attitude that makes your audience think that it really doesn't matter much, then the payoff is much more valuable when the joke works.

Although it is important to build up a joke, your audience should never know you're doing it.

You should never say: "And then the guy says, he says, now get this, here it comes, here's the punch line……"

Tell a joke as if you're telling an actual, true occurrence. Maybe you pretend to actually know the people in the joke. The "lawyer" becomes your father. The cop actually pulled YOU over and this is how you responded.

Don't explain too much. If your joke defies the laws of physics, you don't have to explain why. Don't explain how the chicken was able to carry books, or how a mouse can drink in a bar.

Make the telling of your jokes very matter of fact. The very nature of jokes makes them exaggerated, silly, or ridiculous. Not only should you tell your joke as if it were the gospel truth, but you should also tell them as if the conditions explained in the joke were very ordinary.

Throw your joke away because there's a danger in telling jokes. Joke telling makes you the center of attention. You seem to be asking for it. People are going stop what they're doing to turn and listen to you. And now I'm telling you to throw it all away.

You have to manage a contradiction. You want everyone to listen to you, but you don't want to look like you're overly invested in your joke. It's just a joke. It will only take just a moment to tell. This attitude is important especially if your joke fails. You want to be able to leave it alone with a smirk, as if it didn't matter in the first place.

Here's another way to look at a joke:

A joke isn't a trombone solo.

Know what I mean?

When you were in junior high school, the school band would play. Once in a while, the kid who played the trombone would get a solo. That's great! Everyone should have a chance to have a solo in the school band. So the big moment comes and the kid stands up and points his trombone in the air. Now, that's really nice, but the truth is that no one was waiting anxiously for the trombone solo. Maybe the kid's mom was waiting anxiously for his trombone solo, but she was the only one.

Don't let your joke be a trombone solo. Your joke is great, but no one's going to be your mommy and give you an extra cheer just because they love you so much. Get your joke ready and just put it out there and see what happens. Don't be fooled into thinking that your audience was waiting for you to tell a joke, or owes you a laugh, or even their full attention. You have to tempt your audience, and draw them in. If you appear too needy, if you seem to be begging for the right reaction, your joke is sure to bomb. If you seem confident yet nonchalant about your joke, it will be funnier to your audience. Be more like a fisherman than a kid in junior high school who plays the trombone.

The tickle, the flirt, the temptation to laugh must come with subtlety. That's why we're smug, that's why we throw it away. We don't care if our audience laughs. This time. We'll get you eventually. But please be very careful with your desire to make someone, or a group of listeners, laugh at all costs. Don't let yourself become the life of the party. That's really bad.

The life of the party.

That's what I call these people. They WANT you to laugh for them, they WANT everyone to stop what they are doing and only pay attention to THEM. They go and go and they never want to stop. They don't want to rest, and they're never finished with the spotlight. We're going to talk soon about all the problems related to being The Life of The Party, and how to avoid them.

I've mentioned that I didn't write these jokes. Who did? We don't know. I'm sure someone is going to step up and try to take credit for every joke in this book. But I've seen them all told by all kinds of joke tellers. These jokes have been passed around for years.

As famous comedian Milton Berle used to say, "I never met a joke I didn't steal. I mean tell."

My point? Tell your joke as if it has JUST OCCURRED to you. Tell it like it's yours. Tell it like you expect your mom to come forward afterward and kiss you on both cheeks.

Take a lesson from gregarious people.

Friendly, pleasant people just want to help other people be happy. They're not uptight, they have no agenda. Tell your joke like that. You don't have a big important piece of entertainment that you absolutely need to share. You just have something quick to say that might help people feel a little more happiness.

JOKE SECTION F: THINKING JOKES

I love intelligent jokes. I love jokes that make me pay attention, and think. These jokes prove, once and for all, that jokes are not stupid.

F-1

*****

Two atoms are leaving a bar, when one realizes that he left his electrons back in the bar.

His friend asks, "Are you sure?"

"Yes," he replies. "I'm positive!"

F-2

*****

After a round of golf, four ladies sat around the club house, chatting.

Seeing the ladies, the Pro approached them and asked: "How did your game go?

The first lady said she had a good round … making the comment that she actually had 25 riders. The Pro was a bit perplexed not knowing what a "Rider" was.

The second lady quickly chimed in and said that she had a very good round as well with 16 riders.

The third lady then said that her round was average and that she only had 10 riders.

The fourth lady admitted that she played the worst round of the day and that she only had 2 riders all day long.

The Pro was completely confused not knowing what the term “rider” meant. But, because he didn't want to look dumb, wished the ladies well and then left.

He then approached the kid at the proshop desk and asked “Hey, can you tell me what these ladies are talking about when they refer to “Riders”?”

The simply smiled and said…”A 'Rider” is when you hit a shot long enough to ride on the golf cart to your ball.

F-3

*****

On the first day of school, the kindergarten teacher said, “If anyone has to go to the bathroom, hold up two fingers.”

A little voice from the back of the room asked, “How will that help?”

F-4

*****

Three comedians are shooting the breeze at the back of a nightclub after a late gig. They’ve heard one another’s material so much, they’ve reached the point where they don’t need to say the jokes anymore to amuse each other – they just need to refer to each joke by a number.

“Number 37!” cracks the first comic, and the others break up. “

“Number 53!” says the second guy, and they howl.

Finally, it’s the third comic’s turn. “44!” he quips.

He gets nothing. Crickets.

“What?” he asks, “Isn’t 44 funny?”

“Sure, it’s usually hilarious,” they answer. “But the way you tell it…”

F-5

*****

Brett sat on Jennifer's couch and began to propose.

"I'm not a wealthy man," he told her, "but I will be soon. I've got a very rich uncle and I'm his only heir. He's a very old man and so ill that he can't live more than a few more months."

A couple of weeks later Jennifer became Brett's aunt.

F-6

*****

After a particularly poor game of golf, a golfer left the clubhouse and started to go home. As he was walking to the parking lot to get his car, a policeman stopped him and asked, "Did you tee off on the sixteenth hole about 20 minutes ago?"

"Yes," the golfer responded.

"Did you happen to hook your ball so that it went over the trees and off the course?"

"Yes, I did. How did you know?" he asked.

"Well," said the policeman very seriously, "Your ball flew out onto the highway and crashed through a driver's windshield. The car went out of control, crashing into five other cars and a fire truck. The fire truck couldn't make it to the fire, and the building burned down. So, what are you going to do about it?"

The golfer thought it over carefully and responded...

"I think I'll close my stance a little bit, tighten my grip and lower my right thumb."

F-7

*****

A man in a bar finds himself attracted to a woman sitting at the bar. He is very shy but would really like to talk to her.

His friend says to him, “It’s easy. Just go over and say your favorite pick up line.”

The shy man decided to try it and goes over to the woman and says, “Ford, F series.”

F-8

*****

Two guys were walking through the woods when the come upon this big hole in the ground.

It is so deep they cannot see the bottom and decide to throw a rock down there to see how far down it goes.

They throw a rock and listen for a moment. There is no sound. They decide the hole is very deep and they need something bigger to throw down to hear it hit the bottom.

One of them spies a large railroad tie in the weeds and the two of them get on each end and on the count of three they heave this railroad tie into the hole. All of a sudden they hear this rustling in the bushes and a goat comes running at full speed out of the weeds and jumps straight down the hole.

They were surprised and stood there looking into the hole wondering what would cause such a strange action from a goat. Pretty soon a farmer comes strolling out of the bushes and asks “Hey, either of you guys seen my goat?”

The guys reply, “Uh, yea, a goat just came running up and jumped down this hole”.

The farmer said “Couldn’t have been my goat, my goat was chained to a rail road tie”.

F-9

*****

A lonely frog, desperate for some form of company telephoned the Psychic Hotline to find out what his future holds. His Personal Psychic Advisor tells him, "You are going to meet a beautiful young girl who will want to know everything about you."

The frog is thrilled and says, "This is great! Where will I meet her, at work, at a party?"

"No" says the psychic, "in a Biology class."

F-10

*****

A physicist, engineer and a statistician are out hunting. Suddenly a deer appears 50 yards away.

The physicist does some basic ballistic calculations, assuming a vacuum, lifts his rifle to a specific angle, and shoots. The bullet lands 5 yards short.

The engineer adds a fudge factor for air resistance, lifts his rifle slightly higher, and shoots. The bullet lands 5 yards long.

The statistician yells, "We got him!"

F-11

*****

"Doctor! I have a serious problem, I can never remember what I just said."

"When did you first notice this problem?"

"What problem?"

F-12

*****

A little Grandma is at the Florida coast with her little Grandson. The grandson is playing on the beach when a big wave comes and washes the kid out to sea. The lifeguards swim out, bring him back to shore, the paramedics work on him for a long time, pumping the water out, reviving him. They turn to the Grandma, and say, “we saved your grandson.”

The little Grandma says, “He had a hat!”

F-13

*****

A guy is sitting at home when he hears a knock at the door. He opens the door and sees a snail on the porch. He picks up the snail and throws it as far as he can.

Three years later, there’s a knock on the door. He opens it and sees the same snail.

The snail says, “What the hell was that all about?”

F-14

*****

An FBI agent is interviewing a bank teller after the same bandit had robbed the bank 3 times successively.

“Did you notice anything special about the man? I mean, did he ever change his appearance?” asks the agent.

“Yes,” replies the teller. “He was better dressed each time.”

F-15

*****

A man is telling his friend about his daughter's boyfriend.

"My daughter's new boyfriend works in subliminal advertising."

"Have you met him yet?"

"Yes, but only for a split second."

F-16

*****

A lady called her husband at work. "Dear, would you buy a gallon of milk on your way home?

"Sure." Answered her husband.

"And if they have eggs, get a dozen." The arrived home with a dozen gallons of milk.

"What's all this about?" Asked his wife.

"They had eggs."

F-17

*****

A teenage boy is getting ready to take his girlfriend to the prom. First he goes to rent a tux, but there's a long tux line at the shop and it takes forever.

Next, he has to get some flowers, so he heads over to the florist and there's a huge flower line there. He waits forever but eventually gets the flowers.

Then he heads out to rent a limo. Unfortunately, there's a large limo line at the rental office, but he's patient and gets the job done.

Finally, the day of the prom comes. The two are dancing happily and his girlfriend is having a great time. When the song is over, she asks him to get her some punch, so he heads over to the punch table and there's no punchline.

F-18

*****

Custer was marching his army into Little Big Horn and in the distance they could hear Indian war drums.

Custer turns to his Indian scout. "That does not sound good."

The scout shakes his head and says "That's not their regular drummer."

F-19

*****

Wife walks in on husband, a string theorist, in bed with another woman.

He shouts, "I can explain everything!"

F-20

*****

Jean-Paul Sartre is sitting at a French cafe, revising his draft of Being and Nothingness. He says to the waitress, "I'd like a cup of coffee, please, with no cream."

The waitress replies, "I'm sorry, Monsieur, but we're out of cream. How about with no milk?"

F-21

*****

A photon approaches the ticket counter to check in for his flight. The ticket agent asks if there is any luggage to check. The photon says, “No, I'm traveling light.”

F-22

*****

A Roman walks into a bar, holds up two fingers, and says

“Five beers, please.”

F-23

*****

Bill Olson emailed his wife that he’d be home a day earlier than he had expected. Arriving at his house, he found his wife in bed with another man. Bill stormed out of the house and checked into a hotel.

He was angrily trying to figure out what to do next, when he was interrupted by a call from his mother in law. She was sure that there was a logical explanation for her daughter’s behavior, and she promised to get to the bottom of it.

Bill told her to get lost.

The next day the mother in law called again.

“Did I tell you?” she yelled into the phone, “Did I tell you there was a good explanation for everything? I just talked to your wife.

She never got your email.”

F-24

*****

A linguistics professor was lecturing his class one day.

'In English', he said, 'A double negative forms a positive. In some languages, though, such as Russian, a double negative is still a negative. However, there is no language wherein a double positive can form a negative.'

A loud voice from the back of the room piped up, 'Yeah, right.'

F-25

*****

Applying for a new job, a man asked about some of the benefits. The HR manager mentioned the medical insurance, explaining that the premium would be deducted monthly from the paycheck. The applicant said, "In my last company, they paid the medical."

He went on to explain that a large life insurance policy was part of the package, as well as months of sick leave, a full year's severance pay, bonuses several times a year, two-hour lunch breaks, and unlimited coffee breaks.

The HR manager asked, "Why did you leave that job?"

The applicant said, "They went out of business."

F-26

*****

I have CDO. It's like OCD, but all of the letters are in alphabetical order, like they're SUPPOSED to be!

F-27

*****

Ray had just reached his 175th birthday last week. Surrounded by reporters, he was asked, “Excuse me, sir, but how did you come to live to be 175?”

Ray answered, “It was easy. I just never argue with anyone.”

The reporter shot back, “That's crazy. It had to be something else — diet, meditation, or something. Just not arguing won't keep you alive for 175 years!”

The old fella stared hard at the reporter for several seconds.

Then he shrugged, “Hmmm… Maybe you're right.”

F-28

*****

Two guys driving through Texas get pulled over by a state trooper. The cop walks up and taps on the driver's window, the driver rolls it down, and the trooper smacks the driver in the head with his night stick.

“Ow!” says the driver. “Why'd you do that?”

The trooper says, “You're in Texas, son. When I pull you over, you'll have your license ready.”

The driver says, “I'm sorry, officer; I'm not from around here.”

The trooper writes the guy a ticket and gives his license back, then walks around to the car's passenger side and taps on the window. The passenger rolls the window down, and the trooper smacks him with his night stick.

“Ow!” says the passenger. “What'd you do that for?”

The trooper says, “Just making your wish come true.”

“What the hell does that mean?” asks the guy.

"Two miles down the road, you were gonna say, "I wish that lousy cop would've tried that crap with me!"

F-29

*****

A student comes to a young professor's office hours. She glances down the hall, closes his door, kneels pleadingly. "I would do anything to pass this exam."

She leans closer to him, flips back her hair, gazes meaningfully into his eyes.

"I mean..." she whispers, "I would do...anything."

He returns her gaze. "Anything?"

"Anything."

His voice softens. "Anything??"

"Absolutely anything."

His voice turns to a whisper. "Would you...study?"

F-30

*****

A young lady went to the office where her aunt worked to pick up her aunt's pay.

On her way home she was assaulted and robbed. As the thieves ran away she called for the police.

"I just lost my aunt's pay!" She screamed.

The policeman on the phone laughed.

"Unny-fay, Unny-fay!"

F-31

*****

Police are called to a condo on the golf course and find a woman holding a bloody golf club standing over a lifeless man.

The detective asks, “Ma'am, is that your husband?”

“Yes” says the woman.

“Did you hit him with that five iron?”

“Yes, yes, I did.” The woman begins to sob, drops the club, and puts her, hands on her face.

“How many times did you hit him?”

“I don't know, five, six, maybe seven times … just put me down for five.

F-32

*****

Everyone on a passenger ship could see a bearded man on a small island, shouting and desperately waving his hands.

“Who is that man?” a passenger asked the ship's captain. “Why is he so upset?”

“I have no idea,” the Captain replied, “but, every year when we pass by here, he goes crazy.”

F-33

*****

A Catholic priest, a Lutheran minister and an Evangelical preacher are arguing about religion one day when the phone rings.

The priest gets up to answer it. After listening for few moments, he says, “Yes, I will pass on the news,” and hangs up.

Turning to the others, he says, “I have good news and bad news.”

"Really? Do tell," the minister says.

"My friends," the priest announces, "that was the Lord Jesus on the phone, and he was calling to say he's back."

"Glory be!" shouts the preacher. "What could possibly be bad news now?"

"Well," the priest says, "He was calling from Salt Lake City."

F-34

*****

Two sheep are standing in a field, eating together, looking at each other.

Suddenly one of them goes: "Baaaaaa!"

The other one says,

"Hey! I was going to say that!"

F-35

*****

My parrot died today.

His last words were:

"Dang, I think my parrot's going to die."

F-36

*****

A guy said to his friend:

"I bought my wife a diamond ring."

His friend looked puzzled.

"I thought you said you were going to buy her a new car."

"Sure," replied the guy, "But where am I going to find a fake car?"

F-37

*****

A plane was delayed nearly two hours on the runway before takeoff. When they finally got underway, the passengers were restless and wanted to know what had happen. The flight attendant explained.

"The pilot was concerned because he heard a strange noise coming from one of the engines, and it took a while to find another pilot."

CHAPTER FIVE

HOW NOT TO TELL A JOKE.

Am I implying that you don't know how to tell a joke?

That's exactly what I'm saying. Did that hurt your feelings? Well good, it's about time someone told you the truth.

Holy cow! If I have to sit through one more stupid joke, I'm going to scream! There are just so many of you telling bad jokes that it's just overwhelming. And it's not always a situation where the joke itself is bad, the joke is just being told badly.

Most people struggle a little bit with joke telling and there are a number of reasons for this.

The first is PRACTICE.

Most jokes are told 'off the cuff'. That's the way jokes are supposed to sound. But in reality, when we tell jokes, we need to be prepared.

Jokes need to be thought through thoroughly. Write them down, diagram them out.

But remember, no amount of writing and reading is going to make your jokes funny. Jokes need to be practiced. You've got to tell your jokes to someone, out loud.

Tell your jokes to your mother first. Your mom isn't going to judge you too harshly, but she probably isn't going to get your jokes right away either.

Then try the same joke with friends and other family members. Then tell your mother again. If you don't have to explain your joke to your mother, you're making progress.

The second problem with joke telling is the use of or lack of brevity. Most people drag out jokes WAY too long.

Get to the point.

Make your premise clear, and then SMACK! Hit us with the punch line.

Now, there are jokes that are built around the premise of a long, drawn out set up. These jokes require a huge degree of experience. But joke telling is like boxing. It would be better right now if you practiced, short, quick, hard hitting jokes.

The third problem with joke telling is self-control. People get too wound up when they tell a joke. They want to tell us when the funny part is coming. They want to emphasis how crazy the situation is.

Joke tellers need to trust their audience more. We get it! Or at least we will. Eventually.

Part of the problem of self-control is wanting to tell everybody that we're going to tell a joke, and assuring everybody that it's really funny, and then telling them when the funny part is coming.

So practice your jokes, and stay to the point.

In return, we'll all laugh, and we won't groan.

Start by never doing this:

"Okay, listen! Here's a joke. Okay? Okay? Here goes………"

Don't ever start a joke that way.

You're not running the hundred-yard dash. You don't need to work yourself up, and you don't need to work your audience up. Jokes are best when they are a surprise.

If you're not sure how the joke goes, don't even start. Nothing's worse that having someone start a joke, lead us along, and then suddenly say: "Now how does it go?"

The people in your joke, don't know it's a joke, so make them sound like they believe the premise. You have to believe the premise, too. You have to be amazed by the amazing parts of the story.

Is your joke funny, or just stupid? The only thing worse than a charity laugh, is an annoyed groan.

If you have to explain your jokes, or tell your crowd when the joke is over (you have to tell them when to laugh), your joke isn't working.

Don't belabor your point. Once the point has been made that the hat was red, or the son-in-law was stupid, or the neighbor was old, move on.

If your joke has interrupted or annoyed your audience, drop it quick.

One important way NOT to tell a joke is to start an off colored joke to an audience who might be offended by it. That problem is easy to fix. Just avoid offensive jokes! It's clear that many people today think that funny means telling jokes with vulgar words and sexually explicit content. As a joke teller, you should be better than that. Tell jokes that anyone would enjoy. Grandmas, children, clergymen, everybody. I know that some of you are going to say that your grandma loves dirty jokes. Come on. You know what I'm saying. Don't tell jokes that might offend someone.

Timing is one thing, "all the timing" is another. If you are guilty of using "all the timing" you have a serious problem. Take a rest. Don't tell a joke a minute. Go to the bathroom, get a drink. You don't have to tell every funny story and joke you know. If you do, it means we all have to listen to your stories and jokes again the next time we're together.

I'll say it again, because it's so important: Don't interrupt. Please don't interrupt. You may be waiting anxiously for someone to finish what they are saying so that you can jump in with your two cents worth, but you are the only one. At least wait for other people to finish what they are saying and then, I guess, you can have your turn. Remember what we were saying earlier about the Life of the Party? You don't want to be that guy.

Watch your audience. If they are not laughing at your jokes and stories, if they are trying to change the subject, it is time to stop and think about what it is you are saying. Maybe what you are saying is offending someone. That should usually bother you. Maybe people are not paying attention to you because they are not interested in what you are saying. In this case, go back a couple of paragraphs and review. If you are being ignored, you might even want to check your breath and body odor, though these things usually have little to do with humor. One more note, if people are indeed trying to ignore you it DOES NOT mean that they are stupid (necessarily).

Some of the best jokes I've ever heard are not in this book. This is because not all jokes are right for all situations. And joking at all is not always the right thing to do. Some jokes are for very specific audiences. Some jokes require a specific physical gesture or a funny face.

Knowing how NOT to tell a joke is just a little more important than knowing how to HEAR a good joke.

What's the wrong way to hear a joke?

Well, when someone starts to tell a joke, don't shout, "HEARD IT!" after the joke teller starts. In fact, don't let on at all if you think you've heard the joke before. Just let the joke teller perform. And when the joke is over, LAUGH! Even if the joke didn't do so well. It's just a nice thing to do. Don't pull a sour face and tell the joke teller that the joke isn't very funny, or that you've heard it before.

And pay attention. For heaven's sake, pay attention!

It drives me crazy when I tell a joke, and I get confused stares from people. Then they ask me to go over the joke again, but making sure that I explain each character and their situation and their motives. That's just not necessary. People should be paying attention from the beginning.

And don't tell me you don't want to hear a joke. I'm not asking for much commitment from you, and I'm not going to ask for very much time. Most jokes take MUCH less than a minute to tell.

Just PAY ATTENTION, and don't tell me you've heard this one before, and don't tell me the joke's not funny.

As you might have guessed, I feel like I have a reputation for telling good jokes. Remember the guy I work with who doesn't feel like he can tell a joke, but loves to hear me tell a joke?

One day at work, this friend appeared suddenly in the doorway of my office. He wasn't alone, he had his parents with him. But he wasn't going to introduce his parents to me. He had something else in mind.

"Hey Darrell! Tell my parents that one joke!"

That's one joke? What was he talking about? I was busy. I was talking on two phones at the same time. I was dealing with more than one crisis. It was not a good time for me to tell a joke.

And it was impolite! He hadn't introduced me to his parents, and they were staring at me with grim faces as if they had caught me rummaging through their garbage. Clearly they were not the kind of folks who enjoyed a joke. They looked defensive and unfriendly. I wasn't a colleague who deserved a smile and a handshake, I was a grimy old joke teller, and they were already sneering.

In a moment I got my bearings and knew what to do. Turning around to face them, I rolled my chair over closer.

"That one joke?"

My colleague nodded enthusiastically, and his parents wrinkled their noses.

"Okay, here goes.

It seems there were these three boy scouts and this one-legged prostitute..."

My colleague lunged at me and his parents gasped in horror.

"No! NO! Not that joke, it was another joke! Maybe we should go. I'll come remind you of the right joke later. You can tell it later."

Then my friend ushered his parents quickly from my office as if it was the lair of the actual one-legged prostitute.

I stood and acted genuinely friendly.

"Goodbye! Thanks for dropping in! Very nice to have met you!"

My co-worker kept looking over his shoulder at me as if I were a monster.

JOKE SECTION G: INSULTS

These are just mean, vicious insults. Be careful with them.

G-1

*****

A lady goes into a bar with her goose. Then the bartender comes up to her and says, "Why did you have to bring the pig in with you?"

Then the lady answered, "Excuse me, I think this is a goose."

And the bartender says, "Excuse me, I was talking to the goose."

G-2

*****

Jack was living in Arizona during a heat wave.

“It's just too hot to wear clothes today,” complained Jack as he stepped out of the shower.

“Honey, what do you think the neighbors would think if I mowed the lawn like this?”

“Probably that I married you for your money.”

G-3

*****

My wife found a new way to make money with her cooking.

She’s selling her food to Indians in the Amazon who like to dip their arrows in it.

G-4

*****

A snake and a rabbit met.

Never having seen a creature of that type before, each studied the other.

The snake said, “You have long ears, two funny teeth, and you go hippety-hop. You must be a rabbit.”

The rabbit nodded and said,

“You have oily skin, fangs, and a split tongue. You must be a used car salesman.”

G-5

*****

The girl knelt in the confessional and said, “Bless me, Father, for I have sinned.”

“What is it, child?”

“Father, I have committed the sin of vanity. Twice a day I gaze at myself in the mirror and tell myself how beautiful I am.”

The priest turned, took a good look at the girl, and said, “My dear, I have good news. That isn't a sin - it's only a mistake.”

G-6

*****

My Husband said he wanted a tie for his birthday that matched the color of his eyes - but where can you find a bloodshot tie?

G-7

*****

A couple is lying in bed. The man says,

I am going to make you the happiest woman in the world.

The woman says, I'll miss you....

G-8

*****

A woman was tearing into her husband with just a little more anger and venom than usual. She yelled at him,

"You're an idiot! You always were an idiot. You'll always be an idiot. If they had an idiot contest, you'd come in second."

The man is surprised.

"Why would I come in second?"

The lady screams,

"Because you're an idiot!"

G-9

*****

A man isn't feeling well, so he goes to see his doctor. The doctor examines him, and then asks to speak with his wife. The doctor tells his wife that her husband has a serious, stress related illness that is quickly killing him.

The wife asks "can he be cured?"

The doctor replies "there's a chance we can cure him with chemotherapy, but you will need to take care of him every day for the next year — cooking all his favorite meals, pampering him, making sure he has no stress or responsibilities around the house. You need to give him back rubs, and let him just sit and watch his favorite shows on

TV. Never argue or disagree with him. By doing all this, you'll save his life." When the wife comes out to the waiting room, the husband asks her what the doctor said.

The wife answers, "he said that you're going to die".

G-10

*****

The father was getting apprehensive about the date his daughter was getting ready for. "Are you sure he's a good driver?"

"Oh yes dad, he has to be." If he gets arrested one more time, he loses his license."

G-11

*****

So the old farmer walks into the house with one of his sheep and his wife is sitting there. He says "honey, this is the old goat I been sleeping with".

His wife looks at him and says "see, that's how stupid you are, you don't even know that's a sheep not a goat!"

Old farmer says "well I was talking to the sheep".

This is another twist on a joke that appeared earlier. I include it to show the variety.

G-12

*****

A couple drove down a country road for several miles, not saying a word.

An earlier discussion had led to an argument and

neither of them wanted to concede their position.

As they passed a barnyard of mules, goats, and pigs, the husband asked sarcastically, "Relatives of yours?"

"Yep," the wife replied, "in-laws."

G-13

*****

Bob and Jim walk into a bar. Bob says, "Hey Donkeyboy, get me a drink." The bartender gets him a drink.

Bob says, "Donkeyboy, get me another drink." The bartender gets him another drink.

Finally, Jim asks the bartender, "Why does he call you Donkeyboy?"

"I don't know. Hehaw-hehaw-he always calls me that."

G-14

*****

Bill and Hillary are at a restaurant. The waiter tells them tonight's special is chicken almandine and fresh fish.

"The chicken sounds good, I'll have that," Hillary says.

The waiter nods: "And the vegetable?" he asks.

"Oh, He'll have the fish." Hillary replies.

G-15

*****

A woman gets on a bus with her baby. The bus driver says: "That's the ugliest baby that I've ever seen. Ugh!"

The woman goes to the rear of the bus and sits down, fuming. She says to a man next to her: "The driver just insulted me!"

The man says: "You go right up there and tell him off – go ahead, I'll hold your monkey for you."

G-16

*****

Finding one of her students making faces at others on the playground, Ms. Smith stopped to gently reprove the child. Smiling sweetly, the Sunday School teacher said,

"Johnny, when I was a child, I was told if that I made ugly faces, it would freeze and I would stay like that."

Johnny looked up and replied, "Well, Ms. Smith, you can't say you weren't warned."

G-17

*****

Bob was in trouble. He forgot his wedding anniversary. His wife was really pissed.

She told him "Tomorrow morning, I expect to find a gift in the driveway that goes from 0 to 200 in 6 seconds AND IT BETTER BE THERE !!"

The next morning, he got up early and left for work. When his wife woke up, she looked out the window and sure enough there was a box gift-wrapped in the middle of the driveway. Confused, the wife put on her robe and ran out to the driveway, brought the box back in the house. She opened it and found a brand-new bathroom scale.

Bob has been missing since Friday.

G-18

*****

A local charity had never received a donation from the town's banker, so the director made a phone call.

"Our records show you make $500,000 a year, yet you haven't given a penny to charity," the director began. "Wouldn't you like to help the community?"

The banker replied, "Did your research show that my mother is ill, with extremely expensive medical bills?"

"Um, no," mumbled the director.

"Or that my brother is blind and unemployed? Or that my sister's husband died, leaving her broke with four kids?"

"I … I … I had no idea."

"So," said the banker, "if I don't give them any money, why would I give any to you?"

G-19

*****

A man had been reading statistics about death rates released by the government.

His friend notices and asks what he is reading.

"Do you realize how often people die? Why, every time I take a breath, a man dies!"

His friend reaches into his pocket.

"Well here, have a breath mint!"

G-20

*****

A man goes to see a wizard and says "can you lift a curse that was put on me years ago?" "Maybe," says the wizard, "if you can remember the exact words of the curse?"

The man replies without hesitation "I pronounce you man and wife …"

G-21

*****

A girl giggles and says to her boyfriend:

"Am I pretty, or ugly?"

He answers: "Well, you're both!"

She giggles again. "Don't be silly! How can I be both?"

He tries to smile a big smile. "You're pretty ugly!"

G-22

*****

A pretty girl was talking to her friend.

"Whenever I get down in the dumps, I always buy myself a new dress."

Her friend answered.

"I always wondered where you got your clothes."

G-23

*****

People in England are very formal.

I once saw a drowning man pulled from the water.

The lifeguard rushed over and gave him handshake to handshake resuscitation.

G-24

*****

A young boy came home from school and told his mother:

"I had a bad fight with Stanley today. He called me a sissy."

"What did you do?" his mother asked.

"I hit him with my purse."

G-25

*****

Ralph is heading out to his favorite bar. He says to his wife, Mary:

"Mary, put your jacket on."

Mary smiles brightly.

"Oh Ralph, are you taking me out with you tonight?"

"No, I'm turning off the furnace while I'm gone."

G-26

*****

A bottle collector goes around his neighborhood looking for bottles. He comes to a house and knocks on the door. An old woman opens it up and gruffly asks, "What do ya want?

The man backs up a bit and asks nicely, "Do you have any old beer bottles?"

The lady once again asks, in the same harsh way, "Do I look like I drink beer?"

The man asks politely, "Well, do you have any old vinegar bottles?"

G-27

*****

An artist asked the gallery owner if there had been any interest in her paintings that were on display.

"Well, I have good news and bad news," the owner responded. "The good news is that a gentleman noticed your work and wondered if it would appreciate in value after your death. I told him it would and he bought all 10 of your paintings."

"That's wonderful," the artist exclaimed. "What's the bad news?"

"The gentleman was your doctor."

G-28

*****

A Husband is throwing darts at his wife's photo and not even a single throw hitting the target.

From another room the wife calls,

"Honey, what are you doing?"

Husband: "MISSING YOU…"

G-29

*****

The minister's wife was visiting a member of the congregation, and mentioned, with particular pride, that her daughter had one first prize in a music recital.

"I know how you must feel, "said her hostess understandingly. "I remember how pleased we were when our pig got the blue ribbon at the fair last year."

G-30

*****

A man ran into an appliance store. Angrily, he said to the salesman,

“You sold me a refrigerator last week. You said it was guaranteed for life! But it already stopped working!”

The salesman replied,

“Well, when you bought it last week, you didn’t look so good.”

G-31

*****

A rather cynical fellow was told by his wife that she would dance on his grave.

So he arranged to be buried at sea.

G-32

*****

My dad went into a men's store to buy a suit. He asked the salesman to show him something cheap.

The salesman told him to look in the mirror.

G-33

*****

A woman asks her husband, “Honey, do these pants make my butt look like the side of our house?”

He answered, “Absolutely not, our house is yellow.”

G-34

*****

I went to see my dentist because I had a concern.

I said to him, "I have yellow teeth! What do you recommend?"

He said, "How about a brown tie?"

G-35

*****

Probably the worst thing you can hear when you're wearing a bikini is:

"Good for you!"

G-36

*****

Confronting her husband, a woman shouts:

"Why don't you ever tell me I look pretty? Even my sisters tell me I look pretty sometimes."

"Your sisters are absolutely correct." The husband replies grandly. "You do look pretty sometimes."

G-37

*****

A man went to a barbershop because they were advertising a "George Clooney" haircut.

The man sat down and the barber went to work. When he was finished the man looked in the mirror.

"This is not the way George Clooney's haircut looks."

The barber shrugged.

"It would be if he got his hair cut here."

Chapter Six

Work

We already said that being funny and telling good jokes is like playing the piano, or being good at basketball. You have to work and practice if you really want to tell good jokes. Get ready and commit to this.

Here are some things that you will have to work on in order for your joke to be funny.

You need to get your facts straight. You need to know exactly how much time passed between the first and second time the lawyer visited the farmer. You need to know exactly how many daughters the minister had. If you change your facts, your joke dies.

You need to cut the fat. What information can be cut from your joke, and still leave all the important facts? Audiences get bored if there are too many elements to a joke that they have to remember. Try your joke out on an audience with just the important facts. No storytelling, no set up, just the facts.

You've got to remember your jokes. Don't start a joke if you're not sure you remember how it goes.

Keep a joke notebook. Write down your own favorite jokes, and keep them all together. That way you can study your jokes and practice your jokes. With a joke notebook you'll also have a great way of collecting and keeping track of how many jokes you have. It isn't quantity that matters, it's quality. Some jokes have been told thousands of times. Everybody knows them. That doesn't matter. It's your delivery that matters. And the circumstances.

Do you need a free computer? Well, this one's almost free. And it's not really a computer.

Get some 3 by 5 recipe cards and write jokes on them. Look them over during your day. Reference each joke by subjects that might link. For example, write "kids in school" at the top of any joke that has to do with school. After studying your flash cards, look for an opportunity to share. Even if you have to say: "May I tell you a joke?"

Now that I've mentioned the 'May I tell you a joke' method of joke telling, I want to encourage you to try the more advanced method of joke telling.

Surprise joke telling.

Find a person, a coworker, a friend or family member and just suddenly tell a joke. Make no announcement. Make no effort to blend your joke into the moment with a 'tie in'. Just suddenly tell your joke. This is a wonderful exercise.

Do some practicing in the mirror. Tell yourself some jokes in the mirror.

Watch your facial expressions. Do you look serious? Do you look silly? Are you making the proper face for each part of the joke? Remember, you're playing the part of each person in the joke.

A separate but similar exercise is to make a video of yourself telling jokes. Watch the video and take notes of what you like and don't like about your style, appearance, and delivery.

When you to the mirror and video exercises, you'll experience a confusing phenomenon. You'll watch yourself, and you'll say: "I stink!"

That's an important milestone. You're probably right. What do you do next? You keep trying. You keep practicing, and you tell jokes in the mirror again and you make another video of yourself telling jokes. This time, you make notes about the difference, and how much you've improved. There is no limit to the number of times you can repeat this. Try and try again. That's your motto.

Jokes without rhythm are annoying to hear. Stuttering, correcting facts, pausing to think, all these types of stumbles ruin your jokes.

Now you're going to practice telling jokes with rhythm.

If you turn on your favorite music, and try telling jokes in time with the music, you'll be amazed at the results. Try it with different kinds of music.

I want you to practice in front of a test audience.

Tell some jokes to someone or some people who know and understand that you are trying to learn new joke telling skills. This audience is different from your regular audience. This person or group must understand that you're practicing, and they must be sympathetic, yet honest.

Let me share with you an example of working to understand humor.

My daughter and I recently completed a study on the subject of "getting" jokes. She came up with a way to see how much people really understand when they hear a joke.

She came across a good joke and decided to put it up on the internet to see if people "got it". Now remember, it was JUST A JOKE. It was in no way a true comment on her real life.

So without further explanation, here is the joke that my daughter posted on "Pinterest":

Original Joke:

I told my dad to embrace his mistakes. He cried and gave me a hug.

Following are actual replies that appeared on the internet:

Some got it:

Such a dad joke

Burn

Hahahahahahahahahahahahahaaahahahaha!

HAHAHAHAHAHAHAH OMG

LOL

Oooo I get it lolz

Good one.

Lmao well played

Shots fired

I get it aha… sorry though

HA!

Lol that's ironic

Whale then…

This just deserves a big fat capital F for fabulous!!!

Burn!

I just choked on my tea laughing

I get it

OOHHHHHH

Lol

I laughed harder than I should've

Some had to think about it:

OHHH IT TOOK ME TWO DAYS TO GET THIS OMG

It took me a second

I was like: How sweet… *scrolls* wait a second lol.

Took way too long to get that. It totally sounds like something my dad would do!

Had to read that a couple times

At first I thought this was sweet then I thought on it longer. Embrace=hug. Mistake=you. Lmao.

Wait I think I read it wrong. I read it as you were the mistake and the hug was him embracing the mistake.

Some didn't get it, and criticized me or my father:

If my dad cried like that, I'd tell him to man up like he never did for me and my sisters.

Never a failure, always a lesson. I guess the lesson here is, always use a condom!

You must have been a BIG mistake

Ah ur an awesome mistake. I would do that to my child

You're a mistake. Haha. Haha.

Jokes on you

He sounds a lot like your mom to me.

Some thought I didn't catch the irony:

Did u realize u were the mistake?

So he embraced you?

Were you the mistake then?

For some reason I interpret that as if his dad is embracing him as if he was the mistake…

Some thought the comment was totally serious.

That's messed up!

Things like this will not work on my language. Sincerely the person whose mother language is not English.

I need to take ur advice…

Some were angry, thinking I was trying to fool them:

You're a liar, I read this somewhere else

Fake

LAWL

I would laugh if I hadn't seen this joke a 100 times.

Old Joke.

Some thought I was serious, and tried to comfort me, and point out the irony:

Maybe he hugged u because u were the mistake

Praying for you!

That's the most sweetest thing I've read in a long time. Touches my heart. But you should learn from them! Not embrace! But either way…. This is sooo sweet :')

Some just didn't get it:

Great kid!

Kinda screwed up but I love it!

Amen!!

I love your father!

That's SO sweet!!!

Priceless

U guys shouldn't be laughing that's a really sweet thing to do to a daughter

What a jerk. Lol.

My dad called me worthless once and kicked me in the back of my knee.

Touche dad…

You deserve.

I kinda laughed but I love you

Awe! That's hilarious but upsetting at the same time!

That makes me wanna cry are u ok?

I'm my dad's mistake so he embraced us by leaving. Lol. I think that is more funny than I should.

I wish my dad could do that lol

I would've laughed so hard oh my god

Really man

Mistake one is having a child we all know that having children is a mistake

I told my dad my feelings and he smacked me

Wow. Harsh.

Oh gosh

That's messed up. Call the authorities

It is either a good thing or a bad thing so which one is it?

Excellent advice

A bro to the end..

That's deep

That's horrible

Hahahaha bet he has to go give out a lot of hugs now

Some needed to explain it or have it explained:

You were his mistake so he hugged you!

Isn't that a burn???

He embraced his mistakes by giving you a hug? OMG You're his mistake!!!

Does that make you his mistake? Is this Meg?

So u were his mistake

Oh the irony

What can we learn from this?

Whenever you tell a joke, or make a humorous observation, you never know what other people are thinking. There could literally be hundreds of reactions to your joke.

Joke Section H: Misunderstood

Many jokes are built around two people talking, but not really understanding what is being said.

H-1

*****

A three-year-old went with his dad to see a litter of kittens. When they got home, he breathlessly informed his mother that there were two boy kittens and two girl kittens.

"How did you know?" his mother asked.

"Daddy picked them up and looked underneath," he replied. "I think it's printed on the bottom."

H-2

*****

A man walks into a library and says: "I'll have a hamburger, please!"

The girl at the desk shakes her finger at him and answers, "This is a library!"

"Oh, I'm sorry!" says the man, and then whispers, "I'll have a hamburger, please."

H-3

*****

A little boy sat idly at his desk in the third-grade classroom.

"Johnny, why aren't you doing your work?" asked the teacher.

"I ain't got no pencil."

"No, Johnny." Chided the teacher. "It's I haven't got a pencil. You haven't got a pencil. They don't have pencils. We don't have any pencils. Do you understand?"

After thinking for a moment, Johnny replied: "Well, no, I don't understand. What happened to all them damn pencils?"

H-4

*****

A little old man shuffled slowly into an ice cream parlor and pulled himself slowly, painfully, up onto a stool. After catching his breath, he ordered a banana split.

The waitress asked kindly, 'Crushed nuts?'

'No,' he replied, 'Arthritis.'

H-5

*****

A man appeared before St. Peter at the pearly gates.

"Have you ever done anything of particular merit?" St. Peter asked.

"Well, I can think of one thing," the man offered.

"Once, on a trip to the Black Hills out in South Dakota, I came upon a gang of high-testosterone bikers, who were threatening a young woman. I directed them to leave her alone, but they wouldn't listen So, I approached the largest and most heavily tattooed biker and smacked him on the head, kicked his bike over, ripped out his nose ring, and threw it on the ground. I yelled, 'Now, back off!! Or you'll answer to me!'"

St. Peter was impressed: "When did this happen?"

"Just a couple of minutes ago"

H-6

*****

A man was sitting enjoying a sold out football game, but he noticed that the seat next to him was empty. He couldn't imagine why, since this game had been sold out for weeks.

So he asked the man on the other side of the seat: "Excuse me, do you know who's seat this is?

The man said: "Yes, it's my wife's but she died."

"Oh, I'm so sorry. But don't you have a relative or friend that would have wanted to take that seat?"

"Yes, but they're all at the funeral."

H-7

*****

Two lawyers arrive at the pub and ordered a couple of drinks. They then take sandwiches from their briefcases and began to eat.

Seeing this, the angry bartender approaches them and says, 'Excuse me, but you cannot eat your own sandwiches in here!'

The two look at each other, shrug and exchange sandwiches.

H-8

*****

A man was trying to sell a new act to a traveling circus. The manager agreed to give him a few minutes and followed the man to his car. From the trunk, he took out a small poodle, a Siamese cat, and a clarinet.

The cat began to play the clarinet and the poodle sang out in a strong tenor a very creditable version of "The Star Spangled Banner".

"You're hired!" yelled the manager. "That's a wonderful act!"

The new showman struggled with his conscience for a few minutes, and then he decided to confess.

"I've been deceiving you sir," he said, "The poodle can't really sing at all. The cat is a ventriloquist."

H-9

*****

A girl was giddy with happiness on her wedding night.

As she got ready for bed she made dreamy eyes at her new husband.

"Am I the first girl you've ever made love to?"

Still taking off his socks, the husband replied,

"It's possible. Were you in Pittsburgh in June of 1998?"

H-10

*****

A man sat high in the stands at a ball game, looking down the rows at another man sitting below him.

"Hey, Bob!" He shouted.

The man below stood up and looked around, confused. Then he sat back down.

The first man shouted again, "Hey, Bob!"

Again the second man stood up, scanning the crowd with one hand shielding his eyes. Then he sat down again.

A third time the first man shouted, "Hey, Bob!"

The second man stood up angrily and shouted back, "My name's not Bob!"

H-11

*****

A cop is patrolling Lover's Lane when he sees the strangest thing. A young teenage couple is sitting in a car, the guy in the front and the girl in the back. The guy is reading a magazine and the girl appears to be knitting.

He stops the patrol car and walks over to knock on the young man's window. He rolls the window down.

"Yes officer?"

"I have to ask you, what are you doing?"

"Well sir, I am reading a magazine."

"What about the young lady in the backseat?"

The young man turns to look behind him.

"Well, I think she is knitting a pullover sweater."

"How old are you young man?" the officer asks.

"I am 18 Officer."

"And the girl?"

The young man looks at his watch. "Well, she'll be 18 in 11 minutes."

H-12

*****

One winter morning while listening to the radio, Bob and his wife hear the announcer say, "We are going to have 4-6 inches of snow today.

You must park your car on the even numbered side of the street, so the snowplow can get through."

Bob's wife goes out and moves her car.

A week later while they are eating breakfast, the radio

announcer says, “We are snow again today. You must park your car on the odd numbered side of the street, so the snowplow can get through.”

Bob's wife goes out and moves her car again.

The next week they are having breakfast again, when the radio announcer says, “We are expecting 8-10 inches of snow today. You must park...” then the power goes out.

Bob's wife is very upset, and with a worried look on her face she says, “Honey, I don't know what to do. Which side of the street do I need to park on so the plow can get through?”

Bob says, “Why don't you just leave it in the garage this time?”

H-13

*****

A drunk was in front of a judge. The judge says “You've been brought here for drinking.” The drunk says, “Okay, let's get started.”

H-14

*****

A guy shows up late for work. The boss yells “You should have been here at 8:30!” he replies: “Why? What happened at 8:30?”

H-15

*****

A blonde went into a pizza parlor.

When she said that she would like a medium pizza, the clerk asked her how many pieces she would like to have it cut into: six or twelve.

“Oh, goodness, six please,” said the blonde. “I don't think I could ever eat twelve.”

H-16

*****

One farmer was bragging to another:

"Last summer we had a great crop of strawberries! Big as golf balls! Delicious!"

The other farmer looked impressed.

"Did you put a lot of fertilizer on them?"

"Heck no! Cream and sugar!"

H-17

*****

"While I was in Tennessee I went to a doctor to have my hearing checked. He went around and stood by my left ear. Then he asked the nurse for an instrument. Boy was I surprised!"

"What was surprising about that?"

"She handed him a banjo."

H-18

*****

A boss tells a teenaged applicant, "I'll give you $8 an hour, starting today, and in three months, I'll raise it to $10 an hour. So, when would you like to start?"

"In three months."

H-19

*****

A man rushes his limp dog to the veterinarian. The doctor pronounces the dog dead. The agitated man demands a second opinion.

The vet goes into the back room and comes out with a cat. The cat sniffs the body and meows. The vet says, "I'm sorry, but the cat thinks that your dog is dead, too."

The man is still unwilling to accept that his dog is dead.

The vet brings in a black Labrador. The lab sniffs the body and barks. The vet says, "I'm sorry, but the lab thinks your dog is dead, too."

The man finally resigns to the diagnosis and asks how much he owes. The vet answers, "$650."

"$650 to tell me my dog is dead?" exclaims the man.

"Well," the vet replies, "I would only have charged you $50 for my initial diagnosis. The additional $600 is for the cat scan and lab tests."

H-20

*****

The teenager lost a contact lens while playing basketball in his driveway. After a brief, fruitless search, he gave up. His mother took up the cause and within minutes found the lens.

"How did you do that?" he asked.

"We weren't looking for the same thing," she explained. "You were looking for a small piece of plastic. I was looking for $150."

H-21

*****

A young farm boy at a dance was trying to make conversation with his dancing partner:

"You know, you look like Helen Brown". He commented.

"I know", she answered sadly. "And I don't look so good in yellow either."

H-22

*****

A nurse at the beginning of the shift places her stethoscope on an elderly and slightly deaf female patient's posterior chest wall:

"Big breaths," instructed the nurse.

"Yes, they used to be," replied the patient.

H-23

*****

A lawyer was questioning a farmer whose horse-cart had been hit by an automobile.

"At the scene of the accident, did you tell the officer that you had never felt better in your life?"

The farmer answered that indeed he had.

"Well then how is it that you are now claiming you were seriously injured when my client's auto hit your wagon?"

The farmer rubbed his chin for a moment, and then said, "When the officer arrived, he went over to my horse, who had a broken leg, and shot him. Then he went over to my dog, who was all banged up, and shot him. When he asked me how I felt, I just thought under the circumstances, it was a wise choice of words to say that I had never felt better in all my life."

H-24

*****

An eight year old boy hadn't said one word in his entire life. His parents had taken him to several doctors with no success. One day, however, as the family sat down to have breakfast, the boy asked,

"Do we have any jam?"

The family was stunned. When they'd recovered, his father said,

"Why haven't you said anything before?"

The boy answered,

"Well, up until now everything's been okay."

H-25

*****

A drunk walked over to a man and asked,

"Do you have the time?"

The man answered,

"Eight-fifteen."

The drunk said,

"I think I'm going crazy. All day long I've been getting different answers!"

H-26

*****

A father and son went fishing one day. While they were out on the water, the boy suddenly became curious about things in general and started asking all sorts of questions. He asked his father, "Why does the boat float? The father replied, "Don't rightly know son."

A little later, the boy looked at his father and asked, "How do fish breathe underwater?" Once again the father replied, "Don't rightly know son." A little later the boy asked his father, "Why is the sky blue?" Again, the father replied. "Don't rightly know son."

Finally, the boy asked his father, "Dad, do you mind my asking you all of these questions?" The father replied, "Of course not, if you don't ask questions, you never learn nothin'."

H-27

*****

A man was telling his neighbor, 'I just bought a new hearing aid. It cost me four thousand dollars, but its state of the art. It's perfect.'

'Really,' answered the neighbor. 'What kind is it?'

'Twelve thirty…'

H-28

*****

The judge barked at the defendant,

“What’s your name?”

“Mulcahy, your honor.”

“I want your full name!”

“Full or empty, my name’s Mulcahy.”

H-29

*****

A new farm hand asked the farmer how long cows should be milked.

“The same way you milk the short ones.” Was the reply.

H-30

*****

Two cows are standing next to each other in a field. Daisy says to Dolly,

“I was artificially inseminated this morning.”

“I don't believe you,” says Dolly.

“It's true; no bull!” exclaims Daisy.

H-31

*****

The psychology instructor had just finished a lecture on mental health and was asking the class some questions.

"How would you diagnose a patient who walks back and forth screaming at the top of his lungs one minute, then sits in a chair weeping uncontrollably the next?"

A young man in the rear raised his hand and answered, "A basketball coach?"

H-32

*****

A man took his old duck to the Doctor, concerned because the duck wouldn't eat.

The Doctor explained to the man that as ducks age their upper bills grow down over their lower bills and make it difficult for the animal to pick up its food.

"What you need to do is gently file the upper bill down even with the lower bill. But you must be extra careful because the duck's nostrils are located in the upper bill and if you file down too far, when the duck takes a drink of water it'll drown."

The man goes about his business and about a week later the Doctor runs into his patient.

"Well, how is that duck of yours?" the Doctor inquires.

"He's dead." declared the heartbroken man.

"I told you not to file his upper bill down too far! He took a drink of water and drowned didn't he?" insisted the Doctor.

"No, I think he was already dead when I took his head out of the vise."

H-33

*****

Husband to wife "Would you still love me if I were broke?"

Wife to husband, "Yes, I would and I would miss you too!"

H-34

*****

A divorce lawyer asked a woman who had come to visit him, "Tell me madam, why do you want to get a divorce?"

The woman replied, "My husband treats me like a dog."

The lawyer asked, "Does he mistreat you? Does he hit you?"

The woman replied, "No, he wants me to be faithful to him."

H-35

*****

While driving through the rural area of a state we were visiting on vacation, my mother saw a sign that made her shake her head in wonder. She pointed it out.

"That sign says: 'Orchard for sale'".

We asked her why the sign seemed to bother her, and she responded:

"Now who's going to want to transplant all those trees?"

H-36

*****

A guy tells his psychiatrist:

"I have this recurring dream where I'm trapped in the room all alone, and I want to get out desperately. There's a door, but no matter how hard I push on it, it won't open."

The psychiatrist nods thoughtfully and writes on his pad.

"Interesting. And is anything written on the door? Any message?"

The guy thinks for a moment and then answers.

"On the door it says 'PULL'."

I-37

*****

A guy goes to see a psychiatrist saying he has a terrible problem.

"Tell me all about it." Says the doctor with great sympathy.

"Well, Doc, I just can't seem to make friends."

The doctor smiles and gives an understanding nod. The man continues.

"So how about it? Do you think you can help me, you big fat slob?"

Chapter Seven

Silliness

I've never understood it, but some people don't like jokes and joking, because it's silliness. Of course it's silliness. That's the whole point.

If you don't like joking and silliness, I feel really sorry for you. I think you're lacking in intelligence and tolerance, and I think you're way, way too tense and uptight. You also really get on my nerves if you don't like joking and silliness. But it's your own business and I should just let you live your own life if you're going to be like that.

Even in the most serious of circumstances, and little silliness goes a long way. Of course, it takes a lot of skill to be funny during a serious moment. Silliness is public service. When we say or do something silly, we're saying to others who might be feeling up tight: 'relax, take it easy. Things are going to be okay'.

The skills you are learning from this book are silliness through joke telling. Silly things happen in jokes. Dogs talk. Alligators order drinks. Nuns want to join the Hells Angels. When silly things happen in your jokes, tell them very seriously, maybe with a little concern. Don't make them seem ridiculous. If you do, your audience will quickly begin to tire of the joke. Instead, make your audience wonder with you: why are these silly things happening?

One of the things that makes silliness in jokes work is persistence. The duck keeps coming back. The drunk asks several times to buy the young lady a drink. I'm not saying that you should keep repeating things in your jokes, but make sure that the silly things that are happening in your joke are happening persistently.

How you tell jokes is more than just the words you use. The attitude, the atmosphere, the setting, the tone, all these affect the impact of your joke. If a silly joke or gesture is appropriate, deliver it with confidence.

Silliness is a delicious part of your jokes, but often misunderstood.

People who don't understand jokes think that all jokes, all humor, is silliness and ridiculousness. It's not true. No matter how silly jokes and humor are, they are not about stupidity. Even if the joke is about stupidity, there is something else hiding there. Jokes and humor are about intelligence. Who gets it? Who understands? Who sees the reference? Who's paying attention? Who's thinking? These are the questions that are asked in jokes.

It feels great to be included in the laughter and silliness. But it takes work to keep up. Comedians on television show us this concentration all the time. They have to work fast. They have to be alert and smiling. That's why they frequently seem so silly. They're working, but they're having fun.

This is why Jokes are exclusive. If you understand, if you're paying attention, then you're IN the group. You get to laugh with the group. If you don't understand, if you're not paying attention, then you're made to look foolish.

That's the cold hard truth. That's what jokes are.

We're getting back into the territory of understanding what humor is.

Silliness is one of the first areas of humor we discover in our lives.

It's been fun to watch my granddaughter discover humor.

She jabbers stuff to me, I try to understand, she gives me a patronizing smile, wrinkles her noses and says,

"It's funny."

I apologize and laugh. It's okay that she had to tell me when to laugh. That adds to the silliness. Maya smiles brighter and matches my laughter.

What does Maya think funny is? Maya likes silly things.

Holding her Elmo doll upside down is funny.

Making the toy dinosaur kiss the baby doll is funny.

She recounts things she's seen on TV when people laughed. She points out that it's funny and laughs, but clearly doesn't get it. She's laughing because everybody else is.

She's laughing because she sees silliness happening.

How many times have you heard someone tell a joke, and everyone in the room laughed? Later, someone tries to re-tell or explain the joke, and gets it all wrong, showing clearly that they didn't get it.

Why did they laugh if they didn't get it?

Sometimes someone will laugh, and then quietly ask someone to explain the joke.

Why did they laugh?

Silliness is the most misunderstood part of joke telling.

You might not be surprised to learn that I was a class clown in high school.

One day, a friend from high school suggested that we skip school and go snow skiing.

Mike was also a class clown. He could really make kids laugh. He was well liked and everybody always expected something really funny when he was around. He had been a good friend since my elementary school days.

We had a lovely day skiing.

Funny thing, we talked about everything but humor. There was absolutely no silliness between me and Mike that day. We talked about the future, we talked about politics, we talked about philosophy.

We didn't do a lot of laughing.

The next day, everybody wanted to hear about our ski trip. They assumed that when two very funny kids from school got together, the result would be hilarious. It wasn't. The truth is, it's exhausting to be funny all the time. I'll always remember that ski trip with my high school friend as a nice day spent enjoying the beauty of the mountain, without any jokes.

JOKE SECTION I: DOUBLE MEANING

These jokes are very important, and very traditional. These jokes are built around a word or phrase that might mean more than one thing, and for the sake of the joke, they always do.

I-1

*****

Two elderly gentlemen in a care center were taken out one day for a walk by an orderly named Albert. As they walked, a seagull flew overhead and pooped on the bald head of one of the elderly gentlemen. Albert quickly said that he would run inside and get some toilet paper.

"Albert's a dope" pointed out one of the old guys, "By the time he gets back with the toilet paper, that seagull's going to be a mile away."

I-2

*****

A young boy, about eight years old, was at the corner "Mom & Pop" grocery picking out a pretty good size box of laundry detergent.

The grocer walked over, and, trying to be friendly, asked the boy if he had a lot of laundry to do.

"Oh, no laundry," the boy said, "I'm going to wash my dog."

"But you shouldn't use this to wash your dog. It's very powerful and if you wash your dog in this, he'll get sick. In fact, it might even kill him."

But the boy was not to be stopped and carried the detergent to the counter and paid for it, even as the grocer still tried to talk him out of washing his dog.

About a week later the boy was back in the store to buy some candy. The grocer asked the boy how his dog was doing.

"Oh, he died," the boy said.

The grocer, trying not to be an I-told-you-so, said he was sorry the dog died but added, "I tried to tell you not to use that detergent on your dog."

"Well," the boy replied, "I don't think it was the detergent that killed him."

"Oh? What was it then?"

"I think it was the spin cycle!"

I-3

*****

I bought a dog the other day, I named him Stay.

It's fun to call him.

"Come here, Stay. Come here, Stay!"

I-4

*****

A man was driving down the road with twenty penguins in the back seat of his car. A policeman stopped him and said that he can't drive around with the penguins in the car and that he should take them to the zoo. The man agrees and drives off.

The next day the same man is driving down the road with twenty penguins in the back and again. He is stopped by the same police officer who says,

"Hey! I though I told you to take those to the zoo."

The man replies "I did, and we had a great time. Today I'm taking them to the movies."

I-5

*****

A man goes to his doctor for a complete checkup. He hasn't been feeling well and wants to find out if he's ill. After the checkup the doctor comes out with the results of the examination.

"I'm afraid I have some bad news. You're dying and you don't have much time," the doctor says.

"Oh no, that's terrible. How long have I got?", the man asks.

"10..." says the doctor.

"10? 10 what? Months? Weeks? What?!" he asks desperately.

"10...9...8...7..."

I-6

*****

Every night Harold would watch TV. One night, the doorbell rang. He went to the door and found a six-foot cockroach standing there. The bug grabbed him by the collar and threw him across the room and left.

The next night, the doorbell rang.

He walked to the door and found the same six-foot cockroach standing there. The big bug punched him in the stomach, then left.

The next night, the doorbell rang again. The same six-foot cockroach was standing there. This time he was kneed in the groin and hit behind the ear as he doubled over in pain. Then the big bug left.

The fourth night the doorbell rang. The cockroach was standing there. The bug beat the snot out of Harold and left him in a heap on the living room floor.

The following day, Harold went to see his doctor. He explained events of the preceding four nights. "

"What can I do?" he pleaded.

"Not much" the doctor replied. "There's just a nasty bug going around."

I-7

*****

Three retirees, each with a hearing loss, were playing golf one fine March day. One remarked to the other, 'Windy, isn't it? 'No,' the second man replied, 'it's Thursday.' The third man chimed in, 'So am I. Let's get a drink.'

I-8

*****

My wife told me the car wasn't running well, there was water in the carburetor. I asked where the car was, and she told me it was in the lake.

I-9

*****

My wife and I have the secret to making a marriage last. Two times a week, we go to a nice restaurant, have a little wine, have some good food. She goes Tuesdays, I go Fridays.

I-10

*****

The businessman lay dying, and the priest hadn't arrived yet. "John!" He gasped to his partner, who was sitting by the side of his bed, "I want to confess to you. I stole $74,000 from the safe. And I'm the one who told your wife about your mistress. And John, I sold our secret patents to our rivals for $200,000. And John …"

"It's okay," John whispered. "I'm the one who poisoned you."

I-11

*****

A man rushed into the doctor's office and shouted, "Doctor! I think I'm shrinking!!"

The doctor calmly responded, "Now, settle down.

You'll just have to be a little patient."

I-12

*****

A barber gave a haircut to a priest one day. The priest tried to pay for the haircut, but the barber refused, saying, "You do God's work."

The next morning the barber found a dozen Bibles at the door to his shop.

A policeman came to the barber for a haircut, and again the barber refused payment, saying, "You protect the public."

The next morning the barber found a dozen doughnuts at the door to his shop.

A lawyer came to the barber for a haircut, and again the barber refused payment, saying, "You serve the justice system."

The next morning the barber found a dozen lawyers waiting for a free haircut.

I-13

*****

Two engineering students were walking across campus when one asked, "Where did you get such a great bike?"

The second engineer replied, "Well, I was walking along yesterday minding my own business when a beautiful woman rode up on this bike. She threw the bike to the ground, took off all her clothes and said, "Take what you want."

The second engineer nodded approvingly, "Good choice; the clothes probably wouldn't have fit."

I-14

*****

Two old ladies wait at a bus stop.

A bus pulls up and opens the door. One of the ladies leans inside and asks the driver, "Will this bus take me to 5th Avenue?"

The bus driver shakes his head and says, "No, I'm sorry."

The other lady leans inside and asks, "How about ME?"

I-15

*****

A woman was trying hard to get the catsup to come out of the container and onto the meatloaf. During her struggle the phone rang so she asked her four-year old daughter to answer the phone.

"It's the minister, Mommy," the child said to her mother.

Then she said into the phone, "Mommy can't come to the phone to talk to you right now. She's hitting the bottle."

I-16

*****

Upon entering the little country store, a stranger notices a posted sign saying "Danger! Beware of Dog."

Further inside the store, he noticed and old hound dog sleeping peacefully by the cash register. He said to the owner: "Is that the dog people are supposed to beware of? He looks harmless!"

"Yep, that's him" drawled the owner."

"He hasn't even raised his head to look at me. What makes you think you need a sign like that?"

"Before we put up the sign," answered the owner, "people kept tripping over him."

I-17

*****

"You say that the war ruined your life?"

"Yes sir, it absolutely did."

"But you were never in the armed forces."

"No, but my wife's first husband was killed in action."

I-18

*****

Bob said to the Gym instructor "Can you teach me to do the splits?''

He said, ''How flexible are you?''

Bob said, ''I can't make Tuesdays, but I'm open Wednesdays and Fridays."

I-19

*****

I got in a fight one time with a really big guy, and he said, "I'm going to mop the floor with your face."

I said, "You'll be sorry."

He said, "Oh, yeah? Why?"

I said, "Well, you won't be able to get into the corners very well."

I-20

*****

“Boss, I've got to have a raise,” the salesman said to his sales manager. “There are three other companies after me.”

“Is that a fact?” the manager asked. “What other companies are after you?”

“The electric company, the phone company, and the gas company.”

I-21

*****

Nurse: “Doctor, there's an invisible man in the waiting room.”

Doctor: “Tell him I can't see him.”

I-22

*****

This guy goes to the doctor. He’s got a cucumber in his right ear, he’s got a banana in his left ear. He’s got carrots up his nose. He’s got beef stew running down his chin and all over his shirt.

“Doctor, what’s wrong with me?

The doctor looks him over and rubs his chin.

“You’re not eating properly.”

I-23

*****

“I've really had it with my dog,” said the first guy to his neighbor. “He'll chase anyone on a bicycle”

“Hmmm, that is a problem,” said the neighbor. “What are you thinking of doing about it?”

“Guess the only answer is to take away his bike!”

I-24

*****

The last fight I had with my wife was my fault. She asked: "What's on the TV?"

And I answered: "Dust."

I-25

*****

A new hunter came back to the hunting lodge and said,

"I shot an elk!"

Another guest at the lodge said,

"How do you know it was an elk?"

The new guy answered:

"By his membership card."

I-26

*****

I went to the butcher's the other day and I bet him 50 bucks that he couldn't reach the meat off the top shelf.

He said, "No, the steaks are too high."

I-27

*****

A mother hen was looking at her chicks with disapproval.

They were all messed up and ruffled up from fighting.

"Just LOOK at you! Why, if your father could see you,

He'd roll over in his gravy!"

I-28

*****

A man won millions in the lottery. Overcome with excitement, he called his wife.

"I've won the lottery! Pack your bags!

His wife started to jump up and down

"The lottery? The lottery! But what clothes do I pack? Cool weather, warm weather? Which should I pack? What destination am I packing for?"

Her husband interrupted.

"I don't care where you go. I just want you packed and out of there by the time I get home."

I-29

*****

A hungry traveler stops at a monastery and is taken to the kitchen.

A brother is frying chips.

'Are you the friar?' the traveler asks.

'No. I'm the chip monk,' he replies.

I-30

*****

It's my wife's birthday tomorrow. Last week I asked her what she wanted as a present.

'Oh, I don't know,' she said. 'Just give me something with diamonds.

That's why I'm giving her a pack of playing cards.

I-31

*****

Three visitors in London visit Big Ben and decide to have a contest. They're going to throw their watches off the top of the tower, run down the stairs and try to catch the watches before they hit the ground.

The first tourist throws his watch, takes three steps and hears his watch crash. The second throws his watch and takes only two steps when he hears his watch shatter.

The third tosses his watch off the tower, jogs down the stairs, goes to a candy store, buys a snack, walks back to Big Ben and catches his watch. “How did you do that?” asks one of his friends.

“My watch is 30 minutes slow.”

I-32

*****

A stoner stumbles out of a party, and starts to walk home.

On the way he bumps into a guy who is all bloody and mangled.

The guy limps up to the stoner and says “Call me an ambulance!”

The stoner looks at him for a second, smiles and says, “You're an ambulance!”

This is a joke you tell as fast as you can, with no introduction and no warning. Finish it with a good imitation of a stoner.

I-33

*****

A woman is taken in to court, accused of having beaten her husband to death with his guitar collection.

The judge asked, “First offender?”

The woman says, “No, First I beat him with a Gibson.”

I-34

*****

A man went to his doctor and said:

“Doc, can you help me? I can't stop sleepwalking.”

The doctor went to a cabinet and took out a small box and gave it to the man.

“Are these sleeping pills?” He asked.

“No, they're tacks. Spread them around on the floor around your bed.”

I-35

*****

A young bride and groom were in the honeymoon suite, about to consummate their marriage. The groom gazed lovingly into his bride’s eyes and asked,

“Sweetheart, am I your first?”

To which she replied,

“Why does everyone always ask me that?”

I-36

*****

A husband says to his wife:

“Now, please don’t be angry with me, but I spilled grease all over the stove.”

The wife thinks for a moment and says:

“How about this: I won’t be angry, and you’ll clean up all the grease.”

The man is quiet and then answers:

“I think I’d rather you be angry.”

I-37

*****

A man came home from work and told his wife:

"I got fired at work today. My boss says I my communication skills are terrible."

The wife was very concerned.

"What did you say?"

The man shook his head in wonder.

"I didn't know what to say."

CHAPTER EIGHT

PUNCHLINES

A punch line is what comes at the end of a joke to tie it all together and make us laugh. But a punch line is much more than that, and punch lines aren't confined to joke telling. Punch lines are everywhere. Punch lines are what life is all about. Everything you're saying, whether or not you're telling a joke, is a set up. You're painting a picture with words so that you can make a point. That point is the punch line.

Punch lines are a clearly a part of timing. We've all heard jokes that were ruined because a punch line was delivered at the wrong time, or too quickly or too slowly. There is a stupid old joke that says:

Why can't lawyers/blondes/Americans/whomever tell good jokes timing?

And it's true. Punch lines need good timing.

If a joke is delivered quickly, then a punch line can be fast. Fast punch lines like this catch people off guard. They surprise people. They are unexpected. A fast joke doesn't give the audience time to ponder the joke and consider how elements of the set up are ridiculous.

Other punch lines need to be held back a little for emphasis. A relaxed punch line gives us the chance to think the joke through. Your audience may be trying to guess the punch line. And that's okay, if the joke is meant to get the audience guessing.

No punch line should ever be announced. We don't need to be told that the moment that will make us laugh has arrived. If your audience isn't paying attention, if they're too stupid to understand, then they don't deserve to enjoy your funny joke. Don't tell them when the punch line is coming. Don't clue them in with a gesture, or an expression, or by wiggling your eyebrows. Deliver your punch line naturally, with an appropriate amount of emphasis, or deliver it in an off-handed way if the joke warrants such a delivery. But that's all a part of advanced joke-telling, and we'll discuss that subject another time.

Punch lines are a part of all communication. Any kind of communication eventually arrives at a point. Whether you are giving a presentation to the board, telling about your Aunt Tilly's funeral, or explaining your business proposal to a banker, you'll eventually have to get to the point. It may not be funny, but your communication will have a set up, and then you'll make a point. All information has a punch line. No matter how much filler there is in what you have to say, there is still a point. There's a set up, and a punch line. Anything else is mindless blather, no matter how important you think it is.

That's the great thing that comes from learning to tell jokes. You learn to think about the information in your set up. What does your audience, or listener, need to know so that they will understand the punch line? Are you saying anything that is unimportant? Is some of your information blocking the path to the punch line? You learn the best way to deliver your punch line. Slow or fast. Casually or with excitement. And it's that final point that will make or break any information you are trying to share. There is great value in learning to tell jokes properly.

Of course, if you don't understand your own joke, if you really don't "get" the punch line, it will fail. And don't forget your punch line. It must be memorized, word for word. Much of the set up might be improvised, depending on the setting and circumstances, but the punch line must be absolutely the same each time you tell the joke. Remember what the punch line is, no matter what you're saying. Hit it hard, and then let its impact sink in.

Let's see if you learned anything today:

"What makes a good punch line?

Good punch, ice, and no one is pushing or shoving."

Sometimes your audience knows the punchline is coming, and they have even figured out what the punchline is. That's okay.

Most of the time, the punchline is a complete surprise. That's why it gets such a reaction. It's like a light that has just been turned on, revealing a new perspective on the information being shared (the set up).

Punch line delivery is an art form. No matter if your punch line is slow or fast, you must communicate it clearly. There can be no confusion about what the punch line means because of your mumbling or poor pronunciation. If you have to explain or re-word your punch lines, they aren't good enough, they've failed.

This brings us back to preparation and practice. Recordings, video recordings, mirrors and test audiences will help you find out if your punch lines are being understood clearly.

Even though jokes have punchlines, they may have other moments that are funny. Throughout the joke, it is important that you give your audience a chance to relish the funny parts that come along. But don't get distracted. Keep moving with determination toward the punch line.

Give your punchline and then stop. Just stop. Don't repeat your punchline. If no one laughs, it means your joke has bombed. Leave it alone, let it die, walk away. Do you hang your head with shame? No, just pretend you never told that joke.

Or, you can do a 'Bugs Bunny'. How did Bugs react to people who didn't "get it"?

He would lean against something, a wall or a tree maybe, and he would stare at his victim while loudly eating his carrot.

Then he would say,

"What's up, Doc?"

It's okay if you laugh at your own joke, but wait, just for a moment, for your audience to laugh first.

One thing that a professional comedian has, that you don't have when working a punch line, is a straight man.

A straight man helps the audience understand that a joke has been told.

The straight man doesn't laugh, but he gives the joke teller that look that says he must be crazy!

George Burns was one of the greatest straight men of all time. George would have conversations with his wife, Gracie. Gracie would get things wrong, she would misunderstand, she would be silly. She would be ridiculous. It was all greatly multiplied in its funniness by George, who would listen very seriously, and from time to time look at the audience with amazement and disbelief on his face. But he was always patient and polite with Gracie.

Find a recording of the Burns and Allen show. You'll see the relationship between comic and straight man at its absolute best.

Successful punch line delivery comes from directing your audience to laugh. Deliver your punch line to your audience like a present on a table. Wait for them to laugh. Expect them to laugh. Give them a space to laugh. They will laugh if you make them feel like they are expected to laugh.

One important part of punch lines and delivery is the snowball effect. Always be ready with more than one joke to tell. People will laugh harder at the second joke, because they are primed to hear jokes. The third joke will get people laughing with tears coming down their cheeks, and by the time you've lost track of how many jokes you've told, people will be rolling around on the floor and gasping for breath.

But be very careful with this technique. It is ADVANCED joke telling. You run the risk of becoming "the life of the party".

And last of all we have the "quarterback sneak".

Starting a joke is an awkward thing. People are put off for a moment because they don't know what you're doing.

If you're in a group, and an accomplish says to you: "Say, why don't you tell that joke you told me the other day that made everyone laugh so hard?" Then, you will instantly have a primed audience, and the joke is GUARANTEED to be a big hit!

JOKE SECTION J: TRICKS

Jokes trick you, and that's okay.

J-1

*****

A woman and man get into a car accident. Both of their cars are totally demolished, but amazingly neither one of them is hurt.

After they crawl out of the wreckage, the woman says, "Wow, look at our cars — there's nothing left! This must be a sign from Him that we should be friends and not try to pin the blame on each other."

The man replies, "Oh yes, I agree with you completely."

The woman points to a bottle on the ground and says, "Somehow this bottle of Scotch from my back seat didn't break. Surely God wants us to drink this Scotch and celebrate our good fortune."

She hands the bottle to the man. The man nods his head in agreement, opens it, and chugs about a third of the bottle to calm his nerves. The woman takes the bottle, immediately puts the cap back on, and hands it back to the man.

The man asks, "Aren't you having any?"

The woman replies, "No. I think I'll just wait for the police."

J-2

*****

A woman answered her front door and found two little boys holding a list. "Lady," one of them explained, "we're on a scavenger hunt, and we still need three grains of wheat, a pork-chop bone and a piece of used carbon paper to earn a dollar."

"Wow," the woman replied. "Who sent you on such a challenging hunt?"

"Our baby-sitter's boyfriend."

J-3

*****

A police officer pulls a guy over for speeding and asked, "May I see your driver's license?"

The driver answered, "I don't have one. I had it suspended when I got my 5th DUI."

The officer asked, "May I see the owner's card for this vehicle?"

The driver answered, "It's not my car. I stole it."

The officer asked, "The car is stolen?"

The driver answered, "That's right. But come to think of it, I think I saw the owner's card in the glove box when I was putting my gun in there."

The officer asked, "There's a gun in the glove box?"

The driver answered, "Yes sir. That's where I put it after I shot and killed the woman who owns this car and stuffed her in the trunk."

The officer asked, "There's a BODY in the TRUNK?!?!?"

The driver answered, "Yes, sir."

Hearing this, the officer immediately called his captain. The car was quickly surrounded by police, and the captain approached the driver to handle the tense situation.

The Captain asked, "Sir, can I see your license?" The driver answered, "Sure. Here it is." It was valid.

The Captain asked, "Whose car is this?"

The driver answered, "It's mine, officer. Here's the owner' card." The driver owned the car.

The Captain asked, “Could you slowly open your glove box so I can see if there's a gun in it?”

The driver answered, “Yes, sir, but there's no gun in it.” Sure enough, there was nothing in the glove box.

The Captain asked, “Would you mind opening your trunk? I was told you said there's a body in it.”

The driver answered, “No problem.” Trunk is opened; no body.

The Captain said, “I don't understand it. The officer who stopped you said you told him you didn't have a license, stole the car, had a gun in the glove box, and that there was a dead body in the trunk.”

The driver answered, “Yeah, I'll bet the liar told you I was speeding, too!”

J-4

*****

A big-city California lawyer went duck hunting in rural Texas. He shot and dropped a duck, but it fell into a farmer's field on the other side of a fence from where the lawyer shot.

As the lawyer started to climb over the fence, an elderly farmer drove up on his tractor and asked him just what the heck he thought he was doin'.

The lawyer responded, “I shot a duck and it fell into this field, and now I'm going to retrieve it.”

The old farmer replied, “You just hold on a dadburn minute. This is my property, and thar's no way yur comin' over that thar fence.”

The indignant lawyer said, “I am one of the best trial attorneys in the U.S. and if you don't let me get that duck, I'll sue you and take everything you own!

The old farmer smiled and said, “Apparently, you don't know how we do things down here in Texas. We settle small disagreements like this with the 'Texas Three-Kick' rule.”

The lawyer asked, “What is the 'Texas Three-Kick Rule'?”

The farmer replied, “Well, first I kick you three times, and then you kick me three times, and so on, back and forth, 'till someone gives.”

The attorney quickly thought about the proposed contest and decided that he could easily take the old codger. He agreed to abide by the local custom.

The old farmer slowly climbed down from the tractor and ambled up to the city feller. His first kick planted the toe of his heavy work boot into the lawyer's shins, causing him to hop on one foot. His second kick knocked the man right off his feet. With the lawyer flat on his back the farmer's third kick caused him to see stars.

The lawyer summoned every bit of his will, managed to get to his feet and said, “Okay, you old coot! Now it's my turn!”

The old farmer smiled and said,

“Mister, I give up. You can have the duck!”

J-5

*****

The strong young man at the construction site was bragging that he could outdo anyone in a feat of strength.

He made a special case of making fun of one of the older workmen.

After several minutes, the older worker had had enough.”

Why don't you put your money where your mouth is,” he said.

“I will bet a week's wages that I can haul something in a wheelbarrow over to that outbuilding that you won't be able to wheel back.”

“You're on, old man,” the braggart replied.

“Let's see what you got.”

The old man reached out and grabbed the wheelbarrow by the handles.

Then, nodding to the young man, he said, “All right.

Get in.”

J-6

*****

A man and his wife were having some problems at home and were giving each other the silent treatment. Suddenly, the man realized that the next day, he would need his wife to wake him at 5:00 AM for an early morning business flight.

Not wanting to be the first to break the silence (and LOSE), he wrote on a piece of paper, "Please wake me at 5:00 AM." He left it where he knew she would find it.

The next morning, the man woke up, only to discover it was 9:00 AM and he had missed his flight. Furious, he was about to go and see why his wife hadn't wakened him, when he noticed a piece of paper by the bed. The paper said, "It is 5:00 AM. Wake up."

J-7

*****

A certain private school recently was faced with a unique problem. A number of grade 12 girls were beginning to use lipstick and would put it on in the bathroom. That was fine, but after they put on their lipstick they would press their lips to the mirror leaving dozens of little lip prints. Every night, the maintenance man would remove them and the next day, the girls would put them back.

Finally the principal decided that something had to be done. She called all the girls to the bathroom and met them there with the maintenance man. She explained that all these lip prints were causing a major problem for the custodian who had to clean the mirrors every night.

To demonstrate how difficult it had been to clean the mirrors, she asked the maintenance man to show the girls how much effort was required. He took out a long-handled squeegee, dipped it in the toilet, and cleaned the mirror with it.

Since then, there have been no lip prints on the mirror.

J-8

*****

A little old lady answered a knock on the door one day, only to be confronted by a well-dressed young man carrying a vacuum cleaner.

"Good morning," said the young man. "If I could take a couple of minutes of your time, I would like to demonstrate the very latest in high-powered vacuum cleaners."

"Go away!" said the old lady. "I haven't got any money!" and she proceeded to close the door. Quick as a flash, the young man wedged his foot in the door and pushed wide open. "Don't be too hasty!" he said. "Not until you have at least seen my demonstration."

And with that, he emptied a bucket of horse manure onto her hallway carpet.

"If this vacuum cleaner does not remove all traces of this horse manure from your carpet, Madam, I will personally eat the remainder."

The old lady stepped back and said, "Well I hope you've got a darn good appetite, because they cut off my electricity this morning."

J-9

*****

Two campers where hiking in the forest when all of a sudden a bear jumps out of a bush and starts chasing them.

Both campers start running for their lives when one of them stops and starts to put on his running shoes.

His partner says, "What are you doing? You can't outrun a bear!"

His friend replies, "I don't have to outrun the bear, I only have to outrun you!"

J-10

*****

A woman goes into the grocery store and is looking carefully at a pile of oranges.

"Can I help you madam?" asks the clerk.

"Well, I was looking for some fruit for my husband. Can you tell me if these oranges have been treated with any poisonous fertilizer or insecticide or anything dangerous like that?" she asks.

"No ma'am, you'll have to get something like that from a chemist."

J-11

*****

It was Christmas and the judge was in a merry mood as he asked the defendant, "What are you charged with?"

"Doing my Christmas shopping early sir", replied the defendant.

"Well that's not a crime", said the judge! "How early were you doing this shopping?"

"Before the store opened", answered the prisoner.

J-12

*****

A minister wound up the services one morning by saying, "Next Sunday I am going to preach on the subject of liars. And in this connection, as a preparation for my discourse, I would like you all to read the seventeenth chapter of Mark".

On the following Sunday, the preacher rose to begin and said, "Now, then, all of you who have done as I requested and read the seventeenth chapter of Mark, please raise your hands."

Nearly every hand in the congregation went up.

Then said the preacher, "You are the people I want to talk to. There is no seventeenth chapter of Mark."

Tell this joke as if you're relating a news story, and hit the punch line as if you were accusing your audience of lying, because they probably won't stop to think that there isn't a 17th chapter of Mark.

J-13

*****

A Texas Department of Water representative stopped at a ranch and talked with an old rancher. He told the rancher, 'I need to inspect your ranch for your water allocation.'

The old rancher said, 'Okay, but don't go in that field over there.'

The Water representative said, 'Mister, I have the authority of the Federal Government with me. See this card? This card means I am allowed to go WHEREVER I WISH on any agricultural land. No questions asked or answered. Have I made myself clear? Do you understand?'

The old rancher nodded politely and went about his chores.

Later, the old rancher heard loud screams and saw the Water Rep running for the fence and close behind was the rancher's bull. The bull was gaining on the Water Rep with every step.

The Rep was clearly terrified, so the old rancher immediately ran to the fence and shouted out.....

Your card! Show him your card!'

J-14

*****

A man takes his place in the theater, but his seat is too far from the stage.

He whispers to the usher, "This is a mystery, and I have to watch a mystery close up. Get me a better seat, and I'll give you a handsome tip."

The usher moves him into the second row, and the man hands the usher a quarter.

The usher looks at the quarter, leans over and whispers, "The wife did it."

J-15

*****

"Dr, Dr, I have suicidal tendencies. What shall I do?"

Psychiatrist: "Pay in advance."

J-16

*****

Driving back from Vermont, I stopped at a vegetable stand. It was deserted except for a sleeping German shepherd. I stepped over the dog, helped myself to some corn, then opened the cashbox to pay. Taped to the inside of the lid was this note: "The dog can count."

J-17

*****

A woman announces to her friend that she is getting married for the fourth time.

“How wonderful! But I hope you don't mind me asking what happened to your first husband?”

“He ate poisonous mushrooms and died.”

“Oh, how tragic! What about your second husband?”

“He ate poisonous mushrooms too and died.”

“Oh, how terrible! I'm almost afraid to ask you about your third husband.”

“He died of a broken neck.”

“A broken neck?”

“He wouldn't eat the mushrooms.”

This joke *is from the wife’s point of view. She has a very clear task to perform. That’s how you should tell the joke.*

J-18

*****

A young man was walking through a supermarket to pick a few things when he noticed an old lady following him around. Thinking nothing of it, he ignored her and continued on. Finally, he went to the checkout line, but she got in front of him.

“Pardon me,” she said, “I'm sorry if my staring at you has made you feel uncomfortable. It's just that you look just like my son who just died recently.”

“I'm very sorry,” replied the young man, “Is there anything I can do for you?”

"Yes," she said. "As I'm leaving, can you say 'Goodbye mother'? It would make me feel much better."

"Sure," answered the young man. As the old woman was leaving, he called out, "Goodbye mother!"

As he stepped up to the checkout counter, he saw that his total was $127.50. "How can that be?" he asked, "I only purchased a few things!"

"Your mother said that you would pay for her," said the clerk.

J-19

*****

I was playing chess with my friend, and he said, "Let's make this more interesting."

So we stopped playing chess.

J-20

*****

An eccentric philosophy professor gave a one question final exam after a semester dealing with a broad array of topics. The class was already seated and ready to go when the professor picked up his chair, plopped it on his desk and wrote on the board:

"Using everything we have learned this semester, prove that this chair does not exist."

Fingers flew, erasers erased, notebooks were filled in furious fashion. Some students wrote over 30 pages in one hour attempting to refute the existence of the chair.

One member of the class however, was up and finished in less than a minute.

Weeks later when the grades were posted, the rest of the group wondered how he could have gotten an "A" when he had barely written anything at all.

His answer consisted of two words: "What chair?"

J-21

*****

Two boys are playing football in Central Park when one is attacked by a rabid Rottweiler. Thinking quickly, the other boy rips off a board of the nearby fence, wedges it down the dog's collar and twists, breaking the dogs neck.

A reporter who was strolling by sees the incident, and rushes over to interview the boy.

“Young Giants Fan Saves Friend From Vicious Animal,” he starts writing in his notebook.

“But I'm not a Giants fan,” the little hero replied.

“Sorry, since we are in New York, I just assumed you were.” said the reporter and starts again. “Little Jets Fan Rescues Friend From Horrific Attack” he continued writing in his notebook.

“I'm not a Jets fan either,” the boy said.

“I assumed everyone in New York was either for the Giants or Jets. What team do you root for?” the reporter asked.

“I'm a Cowboys fan,” the child said.

The reporter starts a new sheet in his notebook and writes, “Little Redneck Maniac Kills Beloved Family Pet.”

J-22

*****

A lawyer and an engineer were fishing in the Caribbean.

The lawyer said, “I'm here because my house burned down, and all I owned was destroyed by the fire. The insurance company paid for everything and I'm using some of the insurance money for this trip.”

“That's quite a coincidence,” said the engineer. “I'm here because my house and all my belongings were destroyed by a flood, and my insurance company also paid for everything.”

The lawyer looked somewhat confused.

"How do you start a flood?" he asked.

J-23

*****

My girlfriend thinks I'm a stalker.

Well she's not exactly my girlfriend yet, but she will be…

J-24

*****

"Cash, check or charge?" I asked, after folding items the woman wished to purchase. As she fumbled for her wallet I noticed a remote control for a television set in her purse.

"So, do you always carry your TV remote?" I asked.

"No," she replied, "but my husband refused to come shopping with me, and I figured this was the most evil thing I could do to him legally."

J-25

*****

Why did I get divorced? Well, last week was my birthday. My wife didn't wish me a happy birthday. My parents forgot and so did my kids. I went to work and even my colleagues didn't wish me a happy birthday.

As I entered my office, my secretary said, "Happy birthday, boss!"

I felt so special. She asked me out for lunch. After lunch, she invited me to her apartment. We went there and she said, "Do you mind if I go into the bedroom for a minute?"

"Okay," I said.

She came out 5 minutes later with a birthday cake, my wife, my parents, my kids, my friends, & my colleagues all yelling, "SURPRISE!!!"

while I was waiting on the sofa… naked.

J-26

*****

It was the final examination for an introductory English course at the local university. The examination was two hours long, and exam booklets were provided. The professor was very strict and told the class that any exam that was not on his desk in exactly two hours would not be accepted and the student would fail. A half hour into the exam, a student came rushing in and asked the professor for an exam booklet.

"I don't know why you are bothering. You're not going to have time to finish this," the professor stated sarcastically as he handed the student a booklet.

Two hours passed and the professor told everyone to pass in his/her test. The late student is still furiously scribbling and eventually turns in his paper at the end of class.

The professor says, "Sorry, I can't take your paper."

The student asks, "Why not"

The professor answers, "Because it is late."

The student asks angrily, "Do you know who I am?"

The professor looks at the student and shakes his head.

The student yells, "Do you know who I AM?"

The professor responds, "No."

So the student grabs the stacks of tests, shoves his tests in the middle of the pile and nonchalantly walks off.

J-27

*****

I was walking down the street, and I found a man's hand in my pocket. I asked, “What do you want?”

“Spare change.”

“Why didn't you just ask me?”

“I don't talk to strangers.”

J-28

*****

A woman who died found herself standing outside the Pearly Gates, being greeted by St. Peter.

She asked him, “Oh, is this place what I really think it is? It's so beautiful. Did I really make it to heaven?”

To which St. Peter replied, “Yes, my dear, these are the Gates to Heaven. But you must do one more thing before you can enter.” The woman was very excited, and asked of St. Peter what she must do to pass through the gates.

“Spell a word,” St. Peter replied.

“What word?” she asked.

“Love,” St. Peter answered. “Spell the word love.”

Tearfully, the woman started. “L-o-v-e.”

St. Peter congratulated her on her good fortune to have made it to Heaven, and asked her if she would mind taking his place at the gates for a few minutes while he went to the bathroom.

“I'd be honored,” she said, “but what should I do if someone comes while you are gone?”

St. Peter reassured her, and instructed the woman to simply have any newcomers to the Pearly Gates to pass the spelling test as she had done.

So the woman is left sitting in St. Peter's chair and watching the beautiful angels soaring around her when a man approaches the gates. She realizes it is her loser husband.

"What happened?" she cried, "Why are you here?"

Her husband stared at her for a moment, then said, "I was so upset when I left your funeral, I was in an accident. And now I am here. Did I really make it to Heaven?"

To which the woman replied, "Not yet. You must spell a word first."

"What word?" he asked.

The woman responded, "Czechoslovakia."

J-29

*****

The skydiving instructor was going through the question and answer period with his new students when one of them asked the usual question always asked: "If our chute doesn't open; and the reserve doesn't open, how long we would have till we hit the ground?"

The jump master looked at him and in perfect deadpan answered: "The rest of your life."

J-30

*****

During a bank robbery, one of the robber's mask slid down.

He looked at a man and asked.

"Did you see my face?"

The man said yes! The robber shot him.

Then he asked another man.

"Did you see my face?"

The man thought quickly and said, "No! But my wife over there did."

J-31

*****

How was your blind date?" a college student asked her roommate.

"Terrible!" the roommate answered. "He showed up in his 1932 Rolls Royce."

"Wow! That's a very expensive car. What's so bad about that?"

"He was the original owner."

J-32

*****

A man's wife told him:

"For Christmas, I want you to surprise me!"

On Christmas Eve, the man watched his wife get ready for bed. When he was sure that she was fast asleep, he leaned over her and got very close to her ear, and yelled:

"BOO!"

J-33

*****

A young wife, her boorish husband and a young good-looking sailor were shipwrecked on an island. One morning, the sailor climbed a tall coconut tree and yelled, "Stop making love down there!"

"What's the matter with you?" the husband said when the sailor climbed down. "We weren't making love."

"Sorry," said the sailor, "From up there it looked like you were."

Every morning thereafter, the sailor scaled the same tree and yelled the same thing. Finally the husband decided to climb the tree and see for himself.

"You stay down here, and I'll go up and see for myself."

With great difficulty, he made his way to the top. "By golly he's right! It DOES look like they're making love down there!"

J-34

*****

What do you get when you cross a horse with a donkey?

A mule.

What do you get when you cross a highway with a pogo stick?

Run over.

J-35

*****

My granddaughter wanted to have a 'Cinderella' party. So I invited her and all her friends over and made them clean my house.

J-36

*****

I used to run into this guy all the time at the coffee shop who couldn't remember my name. So, to help him, I pulled a dollar out of my wallet and showed him.

"Bill. My name's Bill. Just like this dollar bill."

I thought that would do the trick.

Shortly after that I ran into him again and he greeted me enthusiastically.

"George! How are you doing, George?"

J-37

*****

A game warden caught a man carrying two buckets of fish from the lake.

"Hey buddy, that's more than the legal limit here. Can I see your fishing license?"

The man shook his head.

"I didn't catch these fish, warden. These are my pet fish. I take them down to the lake every afternoon and let them swim around for a little while, then I call them back and take them home."

The warden shook his head. "I've got to see this. Let's go down to the lake and you show me how you do it."

The man shrugged. "Okay. I guess. They can have another swim."

So the man and the warden went down to the lake and the bucket was emptied into the water. The warden waited impatiently.

"Well?"

The man looked at the warden.

"Well what?"

"When are you going to call them back?"

"When am I going to call who back?"

"The fish!"

"What fish?"

CHAPTER NINE

TIMING

You've heard comedians say that comedy is all about timing? It's true. And it's not just the rhythm or tempo of the joke. It's not just how fast or slow you tell the joke, or when you deliver the punch line.

When to tell a joke is just as important as the joke itself. Good timing will make your jokes perfect and hilarious. Good timing will turn a weak joke into a real killer. Poor timing will make you look stupid every time.

Timing means telling your joke quickly, smoothly, calmly, and with great intent. When you get to the punch line, make sure your listener is ready, and deliver it with the same relish you would muster up to wake your sister and tell her that she has just wet the bed.

Timing means focusing on your audience. If they are following you, stretch it out to really drive home the punch line. If you're losing them, leave out large hunks of the joke, hit the highlights, and then slide in the punch line.

If your audience has had enough joke telling, if they're not receptive at all, it's time to quit. That's a very important kind of timing to learn. Drop the subject quickly.

Advanced joke telling involves great timing. This includes choosing the right time to tell a joke. Mealtime always works. Learn to tell jokes so that you can properly place the punch line when you have everyone's attention, and when at least someone has something in their mouth. Making someone spew food or drink is the holy grail of joke telling.

This kind of timing has been a problem for me more than once in my life.

In college I was on a blind date one night. We were driving to dinner with another couple. I was trying to make small talk. I ended up telling a joke about a man who was hit by a train. The result was silence. I didn't understand.

Later I found out that my date's father had been hit and killed by a train.

Bad timing.

How was I to know? I certainly didn't mean any harm.

Later I learned that this girl would say about me: "That Darrell! He thinks he's SO FUNNY!

Well, yeah.

I just got hit with bad timing.

Delivery is another important part of timing. Sometimes your joke needs to be fast, like a machine gun, or your audience will guess the punchline. Sometimes you need to slow things down, to really draw your audience in.

One of the functional applications of timing is the pause.

Knowing when to pause and when to rhythmically plow through your joke is an important talent to develop. If your audience is hanging on every word of your joke, put in some well-placed pauses. Do it as if you are collecting your thoughts, but not as if you have forgotten what you are saying.

The queen of the comedic pause is the pregnant pause.

If your audience is waiting for the next part of your joke, and they are making eye contact, and their mouths are agape with anticipation, and most important of all: If you can pause without laughing, you can insert a pregnant pause. This pause is an exaggerated moment of silence that accentuates the punchline.

But be very careful! If you don't have the full attention of your audience, they may lose their focus during such a pause, and your joke will fall apart.

If the pregnant pause works, your joke will be unforgettable.

I suppose timing falls in the category of advanced joke telling, but it's not something you can ignore.

One aspect of timing is the 'tie in'. This requires great skill and concentration. The 'tie in' happens when you hear about something that is happening to someone, and then you tie what you've heard to a joke. Someone might share some challenge their aunt recently endured, and you might offer:

"That reminds me of those three nuns and the vending machine.."

So you have much to learn and practice. Timing has so much to do with success in joke telling. Knowing when to insert a joke is a big part of timing.

JOKE SECTION K: CLASSIC JOKES

These are the best of the best. These are the jokes you are most likely to have heard. That doesn't mean they should be discarded. This means that these jokes should be treasured.

K-1

*****

A young couple got married and left on their honeymoon. When they got back, the bride immediately called her mother. Her mother asked, "How was the honeymoon?"

"Oh, mama," she replied, "the honeymoon was wonderful! So romantic..."

Suddenly she burst out crying. "But, mama, as soon as we returned Sam started using the most horrible language...things I'd never heard before! I mean, all these awful 4-letter words! You've got to come get me and take me home.... Please mama!"

"Sarah," her mother said, "calm down! Tell me, what could be so awful? What 4-letter words?"

"Please don't make me tell you, mama," wept the daughter, "I'm so embarrassed, they're just too awful! Come get me, please!"

"Darling, you must tell me what has you so upset....Tell your mother these horrible 4-letter words!"

Still sobbing, the bride said, "Oh, mama...words like DUST, WASH, IRON, COOK...!"

K-2

*****

A lady walks into a drug store and tells the pharmacist she needs some cyanide. The pharmacist said, “Why in the world do you need cyanide?”

The lady then explained she needed it to poison her husband.

The pharmacist's eyes got big and he said, “Lord have mercy, I can't give you cyanide to kill your husband! That's against the law! I'll lose my license, they'll throw both of us in jail and all kinds of bad things will happen! Absolutely not, you can NOT have any cyanide!”

Then the lady reached into her purse and pulled out a picture of her husband in bed with the pharmacist's wife. The pharmacist looked at the picture and replied,

“Well now, you didn't tell me you had a prescription.”

K-3

*****

It seems a young farm boy accidentally overturned his wagon load of corn. The farmer who lived nearby heard the noise. “Hey Willis!!” the farmer yelled. “Forget your troubles. Come in and eat dinner with us. Then I'll help you get the wagon back up.”

“That's mighty nice of you,” Willis answered, “but I don't think Pa would like me to.”

“Nonsense, come on!” the farmer insisted.

“Well, okay,” the boy finally agreed, “but Pa won't like it.”

After a hearty dinner, Willis thanked his host. “I feel a lot better now, but I know Pa is going to be real upset.”

“Don't be foolish!” the neighbor said with a smile. “By the way, where is your Pa?”

“Under the wagon.”

K-4

*****

At a remote monastery deep in the woods, the monks followed a rigid vow of silence. This vow could only be broken once a year on Christmas, by one monk, and the monk could speak only one sentence.

One Christmas, Brother Thomas had his turn to speak and said, "I love the delightful mashed potatoes we have every year with the Christmas roast!" Then he sat down. Silence ensued for 365 days.

The next Christmas, Brother Michael got his turn, and said, "I think the mashed potatoes are lumpy and I truly despise them!" Once again, silence ensued for 365 days.

The following Christmas, Brother Paul rose and said, "I am fed up with this constant bickering!"

K-5

*****

An old cowboy went to a cafe every day for lunch. He always ordered the soup. One day the manager asked him how he liked his meal. The old man replied, "It was just fine, but you could give me a little more bread."

So the next day the manager told the waitress to give him four slices of bread. "How was your meal, sir?" the manager asked. "Just fine, but you could give a little more bread," came the reply.

So the next day the manager told the waitress to give him eight slices of bread. "How was your meal today, sir?" the manager asked. "Just fine, but you could give maybe a little more bread," came the reply.

So…the next day the manager told the waitress to give him a whole loaf of bread with his soup. "How was your meal, sir?" the manager asked, when he came to hand him the bill. "Just fine, but you could give maybe a little more bread," came the reply once again.

The manager was obsessed with seeing this customer say that he is satisfied with his meal, so he went to the bakery, and ordered a six-foot-long loaf of bread. When the man came in as usual the next day, the waitress and the manager cut the loaf in half, buttered the entire length of each half, and laid it out along the counter, right next to his bowl of soup. The old man sat down, and devoured his bowl of soup, and both halves of the six-foot-long loaf of bread.

The manager now thinks he will get the answer he is looking for, and when the old man came up to pay for his meal, the manager asked in the usual way, "How was your meal TODAY, sir?"

The old cowboy replied, "It was fine as usual, but why you are back to giving only two slices bread?"

K-6

*****

A husband read an article to his wife about how many words women use a day… 30,000 to a man's 15,000. The wife replied, "The reason has to be because we have to repeat everything to men… The husband then turned to his wife and asked, "What?"

K-7

*****

Ed and Ted met for the first time in twenty years.

"So, how's life been for you?" Ed asked.

"Not too good," Ted replied.

"My first wife died of cancer, my second wife turned out to be a lesbian and ran off with another woman and took all our savings, my son's in prison for trying to kill me, my daughter got run over by a bus, my house was hit by a low-flying aircraft, my vintage car rolled off the dockside into the sea, I had to have my dog put down recently, my doctor says that I have an incurable disease and to cap it all my business has just gone bust."

"Oh dear, that sounds terrible." Ed said. "What business were you in?"

"I sell good luck charms," said Ted

K-8

*****

A woman walked into a sporting goods store and said,

"I'd like to buy a nice gun for my husband."

The man at the counter said,

"Did your husband tell you what kind of gun he wants?"

The lady answered,

"Of course not! He doesn't even know I'm going to shoot him yet."

K-9

*****

The bank manager was in the final stages of hiring a cashier and was down to two final applicants — one of which would get the job. The first one interviewed was from a small college in upstate New York. A nice young man, but a bit timid.

Then he called for the second man, "Jim Johnson!"

Up stepped a burley young man who seemed quite sure of himself.

"He looks like he can take care of any situation," thought the manager, and decided, there and then to hire him.

He turned to the first applicant and told him he could go and they would let him know. Turning to Johnson, he said,

"Now Jim, I like the way you carry yourself — that's an important asset for the job as cashier. However, you must be precise. I noticed you did not fill out the place on the application where we asked your formal education."

Jim looked a little confused, so the manager said,

"Where did you get your financial education?"

"Oh," replied Jim — "Yale."

"That's very good … excellent. You're hired!"

"Now that you're working for us, what do you prefer to be called?"

Jim answered "I don't care… Yim… or Mr. Yonson."

K-10

*****

"Open wide." Said the dentist as he began examination of a new patient. "Good grief!" He said, "you've got the biggest cavity I've ever seen… the BIGGEST CAVITY I'VE EVER SEEN!"

"You didn't have to repeat it," snapped the patient.

"I didn't," said the dentist. "That was the echo."

K-11

*****

A guy walked into the emergency room and the nurse asked him what he had.

"Shingles." He said.

So she took down his name, address, medical insurance number, and told him to have a seat. Fifteen minutes later a nurse's aide came out and asked the man what he had.

"Shingles." He said.

So she recorded his height, weight, and medical history, and told him to wait in an examining room. A half hour later another nurse entered the examining room and asked the man what he had.

"Shingles." He said.

So she gave him a blood test, a blood pressure test, an electrocardiogram, and told him to take off his clothes and wait for the doctor. An hour later, the doctor came in and asked the man what he had.

"Shingles." He said.

"Where?" asked the doctor.

"Outside in the truck. Do you want me to unload them on the dock, or have them put up on the roof?"

K-12

*****

Fred goes to a doctor and says, "Doc, I want to be castrated."

Doc says, "Look, I don't know what kind of cult you're into or what your motives are, but I'm not going to do that sort of operation."

Fred: "Doc, I just want to be castrated, and I'm a little embarrassed talking about it, but I have $5,000 cash right here. Will you do it?"

Doc says, "Well, OK, I guess I could make this one exception. I don't understand it, but OK."

He puts Fred to sleep, does the trick, and is waiting at the bedside when Fred wakes up.

"Well, Doc, how'd it go?" Fred asks.

"It went fine, just fine.

It's really not too difficult of an operation. As a matter of fact, while I was operating, I also noticed that you had never been circumcised, is that something you want to address? I hope you don't mind my…"

"CIRCUMCISED!"

yells Fred.

"THAT'S the word!!!"

K-13

*****

A man lay sprawled across three entire seats in a theater.

When the usher came by and noticed this, he whispered to the man, "Sorry, sir, but you're only allowed one seat."

The man groaned but didn't budge.

The usher became impatient. “Sir, if you don't get up from there I'm going to have to call the manager.”

Again, the man just groaned, which infuriated the usher who turned and marched briskly back up the aisle in search of his manager. In a few moments, both the usher and the manager returned and stood over the man. Together the two of them tried repeatedly to move him, but with no success.

Finally, they summoned the police.

The cop surveyed the situation briefly then asked, “All right buddy, what's your name?”

“Sam,” the man moaned.

“Where ya from, Sam?”

With pain in his voice Sam replied… “The balcony.”

K-14

*****

Two cowboys come upon an Indian lying on his stomach with his ear to the ground.

One of the cowboys stops and says to the other, “You see that Indian?”

“Yeah,” says the other cowboy.

“Look,” says the first one, “he's listening to the ground. He can hear things for miles in any direction.”

Just then the Indian looks up. “Covered wagon,” he says, “about two miles away. Have two horses, one brown, one white. Man, woman, child, household effects in wagon.”

“Incredible!” says the cowboy to his friend. “This Indian knows how far away they are, how many horses, what color they are, who is in the wagon, and what is in the wagon. Amazing!”

The Indian looks up and says, “Ran over me about a half hour ago.”

K-15

*****

A Man Pulls Into a Gas Station in his Porsche, and a kid on a tricycle starts riding around him.

"Wanna race?" asks the kid.

"No thanks," laughs the guy and drives off.

When he gets on the highway, he sees the kid on the tricycle coming up fast in his rear view mirror. The kid suddenly zooms past him.

"Wow!" the guy says in disbelief and floors it. He catches up, passes, and the kid disappears behind him.

A minute later, out of nowhere, the kid flies past again. Astonished, the guy pulls over, only to see the kid come zooming back at him until finally he comes to a stop next to the car.

The man opens the door to find the kid on his tricycle, wheels smoking.

The kid pants, "Thanks for stopping mister. My suspenders got caught in your door."

K-16

*****

An airplane was flying from LA to New York. About an hour into the flight, the pilot announced, "We have lost an engine, but don't worry, there are three left. However, instead of 5 hours it will take 7 hours to get to New York."

A little later, the pilot announced, "A second engine failed, but we still have two left. However, it will take 10 hours to get to New York."

Somewhat later, the pilot again came on the intercom and announced, "A third engine had died. Never fear, because the plane can fly on a single engine. However, it will now take 18 hours to get to New York."

At this point, one passenger said, "Gee, I hope we don't lose that last engine, or we'll be up here forever!"

K-17

*****

A city guy is speculating with a rancher. “Is it true that a charging bull won’t hurt you if you’re carrying a piece of fruit?”

After thinking it over, the rancher replies, “That depends on how fast you’re carrying it.”

K-18

*****

A lady goes to the local newspaper to submit an obituary. She fills out the form and hands it to the man behind the counter. He reads aloud.

“Harold Robertson died.”

The man scratches his head and gently addressed the widow.

“Don’t you want to say a little more about your husband than this?”

The widow shakes her head.

“That’s what happened.”

The man searches for the right words to explain.

“Well, ma’am, don’t forget that the first six words are free!”

The widow considers this for a moment and then takes the form back. When she finishes she hands it back to the man behind the counter who reads:

“Harold Robertson died. Boat for sale.”

K-19

*****

A tourist stopped in the nearest village, and decided to ask a local for directions.

Tourist: What's the quickest way to the lake?

The local thought for a while.

Local: Are you walking or driving?

Tourist: I'm driving.

Local: That's the quickest way!

K-20

*****

A woman and her husband interrupted their vacation to go to the dentist.

"I want a tooth pulled, and I don't want Novocain because I'm in a big hurry," the woman said. "Just extract the tooth as quickly as possible, and we'll be on our way."

The dentist was quite impressed. "You're certainly a courageous woman," he said. "Which tooth is it?"

The woman turned to her husband and said, "Show him your tooth, dear."

K-21

*****

A sermon is like a woman's dress,

it must be long enough to cover everything important,

but not so long it causes us to lose interest.

K-22

*****

Did you hear about the streaker they caught down at the Lutheran church?

I hear they caught him by the organ.

One of my favorite classic jokes.

K-23

*****

A member of a local parish had the bad habit of taking a Bible home with him every week after services.

The minister didn't want to confront him and call him a thief, because he knew the man was struggling with many sinful ways.

But the cost of the missing Bibles started to add up, so the minister finally approached the man and asked him if he might know anything about it.

"No, father, I wouldn't know anything about that!"

The minister knew he was lying, but let the matter drop.

But after a few more weeks the loss of the Bibles was really becoming a problem.

The minister confronted the man again, and asked him point blank if he had stolen the missing Bibles.

"No Reverend, I didn't! And I can swear to it on a stack of Bibles!"

K-24

*****

One Thanksgiving, two friends were walking down Main Street when a man comes up to one of them and gives him a turkey and says, "Happy Thanksgiving!"

Without hesitation the other friend punches him in the face and knocks him out. The friend holding the turkey said, "why did you punch that nice man?"

The second friend said, "He gave you the bird!"

K-25

*****

Money isn't really that important.

Is someone with fifty million dollars really happier

than someone with forty eight million dollars?

K-26

*****

A guy walking down a street one afternoon passes an old man sitting on the side of the road with a large sack.

The younger guy says to the old man, "Watcha got in the sack?"

The old man responds, "I got some monkeys in that there sack."

The younger man asks, "If I guess how many monkeys you got in the sack, can I keep one?"

The old man replies, "Son, if you guess how many monkeys I got in this sack, I'll give you both of 'em!"

K-27

*****

After just a few years of marriage filled with constant arguments, a young man and his wife decided the only way to save their marriage was to try counseling. They had been at each other's throat for some time and felt that this was their last straw. When they arrived at the counselor's office, the counselor jumped right in and opened the floor for discussion.

"What seems to be the problem?"

Immediately, the husband held his long face down without anything to say. On the other hand, the wife began talking 90 miles an hour describing all the wrongs within their marriage.

After 15 long minutes of listening to the wife, the counselor went over to her, picked her up by her shoulders, kissed her passionately for several minutes, and sat her back down.

Afterwards, the wife sat there speechless.

The counselor looked over at the husband who was staring in disbelief at what had happened. The counselor spoke to the husband, "your wife NEEDS that at least twice a week!"

The husband scratched his head and replied,

"I can have her here on Tuesdays and Thursdays."

K-28

*****

A man walks into a restaurant and says,

"I'd like a bowl of stew and a kind word."

The waitress brings the stew without much delay. As she puts it down in front of the man, he whispers to her,

"How about that kind word?"

The waitress says,

"Don't eat the stew."

K-29

*****

A duck goes into a bar and asks the bartender, "Got any grapes?"

The bartender says, "No. This is a bar and we don't sell grapes." The duck leaves.

The next day, the duck goes back to the bar and asks, "Got any grapes?"

The bartender says, "I told you yesterday. This is a bar and we don't sell grapes."

The following day, the duck returns and asks, "Got any grapes?"

The bartender loses it. He grabs the duck by the neck, and yells, "I already told you twice! This is a bar! I don't have any grapes! If you ask me again, I'll nail your beak to the floor!"

The next day, the duck goes in the bar and asks, "Got any nails?"

The bartender sighs and says, "No, we don't have any nails."

The duck says, "Good. Got any grapes?"

K-30

*****

The sergeant marched into the barracks and called the men to attention.

"Men! I have good news and bad news. We've just received word that all enlisted men are to receive a change of underwear. The bad news is,

Johnson, you change with Smith. Larson, you change with Jones, Brown, you change with Bryson…."

K-31

*****

A man walked into a home store and asked to see some wall paper. After the associate showed him several patterns, the man asked,

"Can I put this on myself?"

The associate tapped her finger on her chin and said,

"Well, yes, but it might look better on a wall."

K-32

*****

A guy goes to the doctor. The doctor asks, "What's the problem?"

Guy: "I think I'm a moth."

Doctor: "I'm a cardiologist. You should be seeing a psychiatrist."

Guy: "I know that."

Doctor: "Then why did you come here?"

Guy: "Because your light was on."

K-33

*****

A world-famous catcher of a professional baseball team was having dinner one night in the restaurant of his hotel. Across the street he noticed a little girl playing on a third story balcony. As she was reaching for a ball that had rolled away from her, she lost her balance and fell from the balcony. The ball player sprang from his seat, ran across the street and caught the girl before she hit the ground. Unfortunately, he threw her to second base.

K-34

*****

I remember the last thing my grandfather said to me before he kicked the bucket.

He said, "How far do you think I can kick this bucket?"

K-35

*****

During a class for beginning artists, one student asked,

"Any suggestions for painting dogs?"

Another responded,

"Wait till they're asleep."

K-36

*****

A lady on the bus is reading a magazine. She comes to an advertisement for a new movie. The pictures shows a young couple kissing passionately in the pouring rain. She pushes the ad in front of her husband and demands:

"How come you never do this to me?"

The husband studies the picture for a few seconds and replies:

"We never get that much rain."

K-37

*****

The manager of a pro baseball team went to the doctor because he had an ulcer. The doctor examined him thoroughly and then sat the manager down for a talk.

"You need to relax. Don't get so excited. Don't get all worked up. You need to remember that it's only a game. And when the games over, you need to leave it on the field. Forget all about it after it's over. Okay?"

The manager nodded. "Okay. I'll try."

The doctor patted the manager on the leg and stood up.

"By the way, how come you let your pitcher bat yesterday when the tying run was on second with two men out in the bottom of the ninth? What were you thinking?"

Chapter Ten

Sarcasm

Sarcasm can be a wonderful tool, if used correctly. It can also be very hurtful and annoying. You should always be sure that people understand when you're being sarcastic. Although sometimes sarcasm is funniest when people don't understand exactly what it is you are saying.

Sarcasm can be a little hard to understand if you're not familiar with the concept.

The Dictionary describes sarcasm like this:

SARCASM. A sharply mocking or contemptuous ironic remark intended to wound another. To apply adjectives to personal expression that is bitter, cutting, or derisive. Sarcastic suggests open taunting and ridicule.

Being with sensitive people is a struggle for sarcastic people because we like to tease like we always do with people in our lives. But be very careful with sarcasm. Sarcasm is pointed, and usually aimed at a particular person. Sarcasm can be very hostile. Some people like sarcastic banter, some don't.

Some people hate sarcasm. People get frustrated with their sarcastic friends because they answer every question with a joke.

"I was only joking!"

That excuse might make sense to you, but it falls on deaf ears to a person who's feelings are hurt by your "jokes".

You may become sarcastic when you feel uncomfortable with emotional subjects, so insults or playful banter spew from your mouth, because you feel awkward and feel the need to balance things out immediately.

Kindness takes on an opposite meaning with sarcastic people. When we are warm and understanding, frequently sarcastic people are really expressing frustration or distain.

Using sarcasm to explain humor, the great comedian Mel Brooks once said,

"Tragedy is when I cut my finger.

Comedy is when you walk into an open sewer and die."

Sarcasm is frequently exercised in our daily interactions with other people.

I remember in my youth, if I got to school late and looked all disheveled. a friend was sure to say to me: "I love how you're wearing your hair!"

Young people live on sarcasm. But there are people who don't understand sarcasm and will believe what you say. That's what makes those people more fun than video games.

When I was in school, our family was having an argument about whether or not I should be asking for a ride to school as often as I was asking. My parents were trying to convince me that I needed to walk more, and I was trying to convince them that all the other kids were driven to school by their parents.

My grandparents were at our house that day. Grandma didn't understand sarcasm at all, and so she was frequently a target of my sarcasm. That's just the way it works.

Grandma asked us exactly how far the school was from our house. I didn't miss a beat.

"Oh, it's got to be twenty or twenty five miles!"

Grandma's jaw dropped.

"No dear! That's impossible! We drive past your school on the way here, and it couldn't be more than a couple of miles away. Why! The very idea! Do you understand how far twenty miles is? Salt Lake isn't even twenty miles away! You could never walk to Salt Lake to go to school! I just don't think you understand how far twenty miles is!"

And on and on and on.

Dad was trying to interrupt her and calm her down. My siblings were laughing.

A joke had happened. A sarcastic joke. At Grandma's expense. Was I trying to make Grandma look stupid? No. I was just relishing an opportunity to be sarcastic.

It happened just recently.

I received, and presented, an attitude of hostility, anger, and insult, all through the use of sweet humorous sarcasm.

It happened when I went to a hardware store to complain about a drill bit. It wasn't working right. A salesman looked at me doubtfully over the top of his glasses and asked me,

"You're using this in a drill, right?"

My sarcasm emergency system kicked in instantaneously.

"No! I've been using a hammer! In fact, I tried hitting it with my hand a few times."

Without showing any signs that he understood that I was insulting him, he continued.

"You really need to use this bit with a quality, functioning drill."

But it worked out. I was now educated. And I had the chance to be sarcastic with a saleman.

If you are truly unfamiliar with sarcasm, here are some generic sarcastic comments that should resonate with you:

- Whoever who told you to be yourself couldn't have given you any worse advice.
- Are you always this stupid or are you making a special effort today?
- Do you want me to accept you as you are, or do you want me to lie to myself and try to like you?
- Don't let your mind wander; it's far too small to be let out on its own.
- Don't thank me for insulting you; it was a pleasure.
- I don't mind you talking so much, as long as you don't mind me not listening.
- I don't think you are a fool, but what's my opinion compared to that of thousands of others.
- I don't want to make a fool out of you. Why should I take all the credit for the one thing you've done yourself?
- I like you. People say I've got no taste, but I like you.

- Pardon me, but you're obviously mistaking me for someone who cares.
- Please, keep talking. I always yawn when I am interested.
- She's the first in her family born without tail.
- This is an excellent time for you to become a missing person.
- When I look into your eyes, I see straight through to the back of your head.
- You are living proof that manure can sprout legs and walk.
- You are not as bad as people say, you are much, much worse.
- You grow on people, but so does cancer.

Now, sarcasm's ugly cousin is the insult.

I know: I have an entire section of jokes called insults.

The problem with insults is that they are usually very funny. But be very careful with insults. Insults hurt people's feelings. That's why we call them insults.

And here's another important point: Insults are not always jokes. Even if everybody laughs that the insult you just delivered, it doesn't mean that you've told a joke. It might mean that you're just unkind.

I see people all the time who are bullies, and who can quickly find something that's not quite right about another person, and then point it out for the entertainment of others who are listening. That's not funny. That's just mean.

It gets worse when the insults are vulgar, very personal, or delivered dripping in hate.

Which brings us to the absolute worst person in the family of supposed jokes.

Vulgarity.

We all know that some comedians get big laughs by peppering their routines with lots and lots of vulgar curse words and sexual references and comments about bodily functions.

That's fine. It's all about free speech.

My problem with all this is that some people come to think that "funny" means horrible swear words or shocking comments about sexual or bodily functions.

I've had people tell me my jokes aren't funny, and then try to demonstrate what a funny joke is by ripping into a routine or joke they once heard that was dripping in vulgarity.

My advice: Stay away from it.

I once heard a famous entertainer tell about a saloon in the town where he grew up. In this saloon the owner kept a pet monkey. On Saturdays, he would let the monkey drink beer. People would gather around the bar and laugh hysterically at the monkey as he became more and more drunk.

The monkey wasn't delivering clever humor, he was just getting drunk. Really, the scene was sad and abusive.

That's how I see vulgarity in jokes. There are smarter ways to get a laugh.

Joke Section L: Silly jokes

Just have fun! Don't over-think this section.

L-1

*****

What's the difference between bird flu and swine flu?

If you have bird flu, you need tweetment.

If you have swine flu, you need oink-ment.

L-2

*****

A sixteen year-old boy came home with a Porsche and his parents began to yell and scream, "Where did you get that car???!!!"

He calmly told them, "I bought it today."

"With what money?" Demanded his parents. "We know what a Porsche costs."

"Well," said the boy, "this one cost me fifteen dollars."

So the parents began to yell even louder. "Who would sell a car like that for fifteen dollars?" they said.

"It was the lady up the street," said the boy. "I don't know her name, they just moved in. She saw me ride past on my bike and asked me if I wanted to buy a Porsche for fifteen dollars."

"Oh my Goodness," moaned the mother, "she must be a child abuser. Who knows what she will do next? John, you go right up there and see what's going on."

So the boy's father walked up the street to the house where the lady lived and found her out in the yard calmly planting petunias! He introduced himself as the father of the boy to whom she had sold a Porsche for fifteen dollars and demanded to know why she did it.

"Well," she said, "this morning I got a phone call from my husband. I thought he was on a business trip, but learned from a friend he has run off to Hawaii with his secretary and really doesn't intend to come back. He claimed he was stranded and asked me to sell his new Porsche and send him the money. So I did."

L-3

*****

There once was a scientist who studied frogs. One day, the scientist put the frog on the ground and told it to jump. The frog jumped four feet.

So the scientist wrote in his notebook, "Frog with four feet, jumps four feet."

So the scientist cut off one of one of the frog's legs. The scientist told the frog to jump. Frog jumped three feet. So the scientist wrote in his note book, "Frog with three feet, jumps three feet."

So the scientist cut of another leg. He told the frog to jump. The frog jumped two feet. So the scientist wrote in his notebook "Frog with two feet, jumps two feet."

The scientist cut off one more leg. He told the frog to jump. Frog jumped one foot. So the scientist wrote in his notebook, "Frog with one foot, jumps one foot."

So the scientist cut off his last leg.

"He said, "Frog jump. Frog jump. FROG JUMP!"

So the scientist wrote in his notebook, "Frog with no feet, goes deaf."

L-4

*****

There was this guy at a bar, just looking at his drink. He stays like that for half of an hour.

Then, this big trouble-making truck driver steps next to him, takes the drink from the guy, and just drinks it all down. The poor man starts crying. The truck driver says, “Come on man, I was just joking. Here, I'll buy you another drink. I just can't stand to see a man cry.”

“No, it's not that. This day is the worst of my life. First, I fall asleep, and I go late to my office. My boss, outrageous, fires me. When I leave the building, to my car, I found out it was stolen. The police said that they can do nothing. I get a cab to return home, and when I leave it, I remember I left my wallet and credit cards there. The cab driver just drives away.”

“I go home, and when I get there, I find my wife in bed with the gardener. I leave home, and come to this bar. And just when I was thinking about putting an end to my life, you show up and drink my poison.”

L-5

*****

A man and a woman, who have never met before, find themselves assigned to the

same sleeping room on a transcontinental train.

Though initially embarrassed and uneasy over sharing a room, the two are

tired and fall asleep quickly…he in the upper bunk and she in the lower.

At 1:00 AM, he leans over and gently wakes the woman saying, “Ma'am, I'm sorry to bother you, but would you be willing to reach into the closet to get me a second blanket? I'm awfully cold."

"I have a better idea," she replies. "Just for tonight, let's pretend that we're married."

"Wow! That's a great idea!!" he exclaims.

"Good," she replies. "Get your own damn blanket!"

After a moment of silence, he farted.

L-6

*****

While attending a Marriage Seminar dealing with communication, Tom and his wife Grace listened to the instructor,

"It is essential that husbands and wives know each other's likes and dislikes."

He addressed the man, "Can you name your wife's favorite flower?"

Tom leaned over, touched his wife's arm gently and whispered, "It's Pillsbury, isn't it?"

L-7

*****

Q: When does a person decide to become an accountant?

A: When he realizes he doesn't have the charisma to succeed as an undertaker

L-8

*****

Employer to applicant: "In this job we need someone who is responsible."

Applicant: "I'm the one you want.

On my last job, every time anything went wrong, they said I was responsible."

L-9

*****

A man put some red candies in his shirt pocket. Because of the unseasonably hot weather, the candy melted and left a large, round, red stain on his shirt.

His wife took the shirt to the dry cleaners, and the laundry man looked it over. He was impressed and nodded,

"Good shot," he said.

L-10

*****

"I'm going to get a divorce," the man told his friend. "My wife hasn't spoken to me in three months."

"I'd think twice about that if I were you," his friend said. "Wives like that are hard to find."

L-11

*****

A husband says to his wife,

"Honey, I've been thinking it over since that fight we had, and I've realized that everything you said was true. You were right, and I was wrong."

The wife snapped angrily,

"Well it's too late now, I've changed my mind!"

L-12

*****

Two friends were chatting.

"Which would you rather be in – an explosion, or a collision?"

The second friend smiled.

"In a collision, anytime!"

The first friend was curious,

"Why?" he asked.

"Well, because in a collision, there you are. But in an explosion, where are you?"

L-13

*****

Buddha walks into a pizza joint and says, "Make me one with everything."

Cashier: "That'll be $9.50"

Buddha hands him a ten. Waits. Waits. He says, "Where's my change?"

Cashier replies, "Change must come from within"

L-14

*****

A lady opened her refrigerator and saw a rabbit sitting on one of the shelves.

“What are you doing in there?” she asked.

The rabbit replied: “This is a Westinghouse, isn't it?”

The lady replied “Yes.”

“Well,” the rabbit said, “I'm westing”.

L-15

*****

A wife was complaining about her husband.

“He’s says he’s writing a novel. I don’t know why. He could stop by the bookstore and buy one for eight dollars.”

L-16

*****

A lady says to her husband, “Did you see those soldiers looking at that girl in the halter top?”

Her husband replies, “What soldiers?”

L-17

*****

On the job the boss is watching his workers carry buckets of water. Everyone is carrying two buckets except for one guy.

“Hey! How come you’re only carrying one bucket, and not two like everybody else?”

“Well, I guess those other guys are too lazy to make two trips.”

L-18

*****

A construction worker walks into a bar. He's a rather large, menacing guy. He orders a beer, chugs it back, and bellows, "All you guys on this side of the bar are a bunch of idiots!" A sudden silence descends. After a moment, he asks, "Anyone got a problem with that?" The silence lengthens.

He then chugs back another beer, and growls, "And all you guys on the other side of the bar are scum!" Once again, the bar is silent. He looks around belligerently, and roars, "Anyone got a problem with that?"

A lone man gets up from his stool, and starts to walk towards the construction worker who yells, "You got a problem, buddy?"

The man replies, "Oh no. I'm just on the wrong side of the bar."

L-19

*****

A young man was bragging to a friend.

"Hey, guess what! I just got engaged to a girl over in Centerville!"

"That's great!" replied the friend. "What wait a minute, aren't you engaged to a girl from Farmington?"

"That's right, I am!" beamed the young man.

"Hang on a minute, how can you be engaged to two girls in two different towns?"

The young man smiled confidently. "I've got a bicycle."

L-20

*****

A young Dentist had just started his own Clinic. He rented a beautiful office and had it furnished with antiques.

Sitting there, he saw a man come into the front office. Wishing to appear the "busy dentist", the dentist picked up the phone and started to pretend he had to give an appointment. Finally he hung up and asked the visitor, "Can I help you?"

The man said, "Yeah, I've come to activate the phone"

L-21

*****

A pretty young woman at the farmer's market asked the male vendor the price of his apples. He winked at her and said, "One kiss each."

The young woman paused, then smiled and asked for a dozen.

The vendor gladly complied. Upon handing over the produce, he declared that he was owed a dozen kisses.

The young woman winked at him, and pointed to the elderly gentleman behind her.

"Grandpa's paying," she said.

L-22

*****

What's the definition of a gentleman?

A man who knows how to play the accordion, but doesn't.

L-23

*****

My wife and I attended a program put on by an Indian school from North Dakota.

They gave her an Indian Name: "Five Horses"

or in English "Nag, nag, nag, nag, nag."

L-24

*****

A giraffe walks into a bar and lies down to take a nap.

A drunk wanders in and asks the bartender, "What's this lyin' here?"

The bartender replies, "That's no lion, that's a giraffe!"

L-25

*****

Two old ladies are in a restaurant. One complains, "You know, the food here is just terrible."

The other shakes her head and adds, "And such small portions."

L-26

*****

There were three little boys visiting their grandparents.

The oldest came out and asked his grandpa, "Can you make a sound like a frog, Grandpappy? Grandpa responds, "No, I don't really want to make the sound of a frog now."

So, the second little boy comes out and asks his grandfather, "Will you please make a sound like a frog?"

Grandpa again says, “No, not now. I don't really want to do that. I’m in a grumpy mood. Maybe later.”

Then the third little boy comes out and says, “Grandpa, oh please…Please, please will you make a sound like a frog?”

“Why do all of you boys want me to make a sound like a frog?” Grandpa asked.

The little boy replied with a hopeful face, “Well, Mom said that when you croak, we get to go to Disney World!”

L-27

*****

The inmate on death row was scheduled to be put to death by firing squad the follow morning. When the prison guards asked him if he wanted something specific for his last meal, he didn't want anything special.

When they asked if there was something special he wanted to do, he said nothing.

Finally when he was put before the firing squad, the guard asked if he wanted a cigarette and a blindfold.

“No,” the inmate said, “just get it over with.”

“Well, is there anything that I can do for you before you go?” said the guard.

The inmate thought. “Actually,” he said, “Music is my life. One thing I would really like, is to sing my favorite song, the whole thing, with no interruptions.”

The warden nodded to the guard and the guard told the prisoner to go ahead.

The inmate started, “One billion bottles of beer on the wall…”

L-28

*****

How I learned to mind my own business: I was walking past the mental hospital the other day, and I could hear all the patients shouting, "13! 13! 13!"

The fence was too high to see over, but I saw a little gap in the planks, so I looked through to see what was going on. Someone poked me in the eye with a stick!

Then they all started shouting, "14! 14! 14!"

L-29

*****

A wife was making a breakfast of fried eggs for her husband. Suddenly, her husband burst into the kitchen.

"Careful," he said, "CAREFUL! Put in some more butter! Oh my gosh! You're cooking too many at once. TOO MANY! Turn them! TURN THEM NOW! We need more butter. Oh my gosh! WHERE are we going to get MORE BUTTER? They're going to STICK! Careful. CAREFUL! I said be CAREFUL! You NEVER listen to me when you're cooking! Never! Turn them! Hurry up! Are you CRAZY? Have you LOST your mind? Don't forget to salt them. You know you always forget to salt them. Use the! Salt. USE THE SALT! THE SALT!"

The wife stared at him. "What in the world is wrong with you? You think I don't know how to fry a couple of eggs?"

The husband calmly replied, "I just wanted to show you what it feels like when I'm driving."

L-30

*****

After the surgery, the doctor apologized to his patient.

"I've got good news and bad news for you.

I accidentally amputated your good leg. So we had to amputate your infected leg as well."

The patient was horrified.

"What in the world is the good news?"

"The janitor wants to buy your shoes!"

L-31

*****

A woman came to her doctor in a panic.

"Doctor, all day long my daughter eats yeast and car wax, and won't get out of bed! What will happen to her?"

"Don't worry," said the Doctor, "eventually she will rise and shine."

L-32

*****

An 85-year-old widow went on a blind date with a 90-year-old man.

When she returned to her daughter's house later that night, she seemed upset.

"What happened, Mother?" the daughter asked.

"I had to slap his face three times!"

"You mean he got fresh?"

"No," she answered. "I thought he was dead!"

L-33

*****

A Man walks out to the street and catches a taxi just going by. He gets into the taxi, and the cabbie says, 'Perfect timing. You're just like Frank.'

Passenger: 'Who?'

Cabbie: 'Frank Feldman. He's a guy who did everything right all the time. Like my coming along when you needed a cab, things happened like that to Frank Feldman every single time.'

Passenger: 'There are always a few clouds over everybody.'

Cabbie: 'Not Frank Feldman. He was a terrific athlete. He could have won the Grand-Slam at tennis. He could golf with the pros. He sang like an opera baritone and danced like a Broadway star and you should have heard him play the piano. He was an amazing guy.'

Passenger: 'Sounds like he was something really special.'

Cabbie: 'There's more… He had a memory like a computer. He remembered everybody's birthday. He knew all about wine, which foods to order and which fork to eat them with. He could fix anything. Not like me. I change a fuse, and the whole street blacks out. But Frank Feldman, he could do everything right.'

Passenger: 'Wow, some guy then.'

Cabbie: 'He always knew the quickest way to go in traffic and avoid traffic jams Not like me, I always seem to get stuck in them. But Frank, he never made a mistake, and he really knew how to treat a woman and make her feel good. He would never answer her back even if she was in the wrong; and his clothing was always immaculate, shoes highly polished too - He was the perfect man! He never made a mistake. No one could ever measure up to Frank Feldman.'

Passenger: 'An amazing fellow. How did you meet him?'

Cabbie: 'Well, I never actually met Frank, he died.

I married his widow.

L-34

*****

A woman in labor suddenly shouted, “Shouldn’t! Wouldn’t! Couldn’t! Didn’t! Can’t!”

“Don’t worry,” said the doc. “Those are just contractions.”

L-35

*****

This hillbilly is traveling down the road when a highway patrolman pulls him over.

“You got any I.D.?” the patrolman asks.

“Bout what?” the hillbilly replies.

L-35

*****

A guitar student said to his instructor: “I really don’t like the sound of my own guitar playing.”

The instructor nodded thoughtfully. “That actually more common than you know.”

The student perked up: “Oh really?”

“Sure!” responded the guitar instructor. “I’ve heard lots of people say that they don’t like the sound of your guitar playing.”

CHAPTER ELEVEN

THE TRUTH

Now we'll discuss the most difficult rule of humor of all. Some jokes are funny just because they're true. And many true things are funny. If something is funny because it's true, most of the time that truth is painful or embarrassing. That bothers some people, but that's just the way it is. The truth can be very funny.

People ask me why jokes are made about true things at all. Why make fun of someone's misfortune or embarrassment?

Humor brings truth to light. Jokes offer another point of view on the truth. Humor can calm things down when people are upset.

The truth can cause discomfort, and discomfort is one of the key elements of humor.

For example, if we narrowly avoid bumping into another person in a hallway, we laugh. Why do we do that? Understanding the truth about what could have been embarrassing or painful makes us laugh. Jokes that deal in truth make us laugh for the same reason.

Many jokes are born from true incidents that all of us can understand and enjoy. Comedians on TV are always talking about true things that make us laugh. We call it "observational comedy". Just last night after watching comedians on TV, I noticed that:

Women's magazines contain equal amounts of articles about the importance of accepting yourself just as you are, and articles about how to lose ten pounds in two months.

People press harder on the buttons on the remote control when the batteries are dying.

We like to say that we "slept like a baby", but babies wake up crying every two hours

A bank is a place that will loan you money, if you can prove that you don't need it.

Sometimes I interact with people who say really funny things, but that's not their intention. They're just telling the truth as they see it.

Humorous truth comes mostly from anecdotal incidents. This is the pinnacle of my sense of humor. Jokes and joking have defined my relationships with people who are close to me. I've always felt that my purpose in this life has been to help people through difficult things through humor. Some personal examples:

In school there were always kids with acne. School kids see classmates with zits, and they say things. Right? It's just the truth.

One kid in particular use to give kids a really hard time. He told all the acne kids that they had zits because they were dirty.

But later that summer, this bully was hit by the worst acne I've ever seen. A group of us ran into him at a park. Most of us pretended not to notice his really severe acne. But one of the group got some revenge.

"Hey, Bill! What happened to your face? It looks like it caught on fire and someone tried to put it out with a pitch fork!"

A joke? Kind of. Inappropriate? Probably.

"I was just joking!" That was the defense

But wasn't that the truth?

Bill stormed off angrily, and everyone who had heard the comment burst into hilarious laughter. Why? Why was Bill angry? Why was everyone laughing? It was all true, wasn't it? That's the rub. True things are funny. But they are very dangerous. If you can learn to joke safely about true things you will have reached the pinnacle of humor.

More recently I worked in an office with a young lady named Gayleen. Gayleen was very ugly. That's just the truth. She was shy and awkward. But Gayleen was seeking romance. She was corresponding with a young man in England. This young man was coming to the US to meet Gayleen, and they had talked about marriage.

One day at work, Gayleen started to cry: "Just look at me! He's going to be so disappointed when he see me! He's going to take one look at my hair, and my glasses and my teeth and my complexion, and he's going to get right back on that boat for England."

I decided that it was important to say something. "Oh Gayleen, don't say that! It's not true! He'll probably come over on an airplane."

Gayleen left the room in tears and everyone chastised me for teasing her. "No one should say anything! It's none of our business!"

But when Gayleen came back, she wanted more comments on her situation. A group discussion started up with everyone making suggestions about what Gayleen could do to improve her appearance. It was funny. We laughed really hard. Gayleen cried about it. But you should see her wedding pictures. She told everyone who came to her reception: "Hi, I'm Gayleen, and I used to be ugly!" Cruel, true jokes lead to a dramatic change in Gayleen.

Recently my wife and I were walking our dog. We stopped to chat with some neighbors. We don't know them very well, so we were taking the opportunity to let everyone share something about their family.

On older gentleman went on and on about his family, and how much he loved them. When he finished his roll, I made a comment:

"You must have a very lovely wife."

His answer: "Nope."

I was shaken. "I'm so sorry. I got the impression that your wife was living." Without the slightest indication that he was trying to be funny, he said,

"She IS living, she's just not lovely."

There is a truth about Jokes and humor that is uncomfortable.

I was at a dinner party with some good friends. For years my friend has complained to me that his wife hates jokes.

What else is true?

You've got something to contribute to this search for humor. We'll all understand and use jokes better if you will join in with us and share your thoughts. I want you to contribute and participate in our discussions. Please visit our facebook page: You Must Be Joking.

Or visit my blog: www.youtellajoke.blogspot .com

Or follow me on twitter @teachaman

And you should visit Tyson Cole's site. He's the artist who did my book cover.

http://thedeepend-comic.blogspot.com/

All very true.

Share your favorite jokes with us. Leave your thoughts about what you think funny means. We'd love to hear from you!

Anything else true?

I speak to groups about humor and joke telling. I would love to speak to your group about these subjects that are so dear to my heart. Contact me! I'll come visit your group and we'll have a great time! We'll tell a lot of jokes, and we'll learn something about effective communication.

JOKE SECTION M: JOKES THAT I'M WORKING ON.

I'm learning and practicing these jokes.

M-1

*****

A man named Markowitz was vacationing on a cruise ship. Assigned to his table in the dining room was a French man. The first night the French man sat at the table, smiled, and said, "Bon Appetit".

Markowitz nodded awkwardly and said, "Markowitz".

For two days, breakfast lunch and dinner, the scene repeated. The French man would sit and say, "Bon Appetit", and Markowitz would nod and say, "Markowitz".

Finally on the third day, Markowitz mentioned it to another passenger.

"You've misunderstood. "Bon Appetit" is not the man's name. It's the way French people invite you to enjoy your meal.

Embarrassed but encouraged, Markowitz went to dinner. As the French man sat down, Markowitz quickly smiled and said, "Bon Appetit".

The French man nodded, smiled, and said, "Markowitz".

M-2

*****

The plumber knocked on the door and a lady answered.

"Where's the drip?" He asked pleasantly.

The lady gestured over her shoulder.

"He's in the basement, trying to fix the leak."

M-3

*****

A lady walked into a boutique and asked the sales lady "May I try on that cute dress in the window?"

The sales lady replied, "Sure, but wouldn't you be more comfortable in a dressing room?"

M-4

*****

A man came home one night and found his wife in tears because the dog had eaten one of her chicken pot pies.

"Don't worry," said the man. "Stop crying, I'll buy you another dog."

M-5

*****

The old maid gathered her robe closed up to her neck as the burglar approached her.

"Don't scream lady, I just want your money."

The spinster sneered,

"You're just like all the other men!"

M-6

*****

A murderer, sitting in the electric chair, was about to be executed.

"Have you any last requests?" Asked the chaplain.

"Yes," replied the murderer. "Will you hold my hand?"

M-7

*****

A boy was standing on the street corner, selling newspapers.

"Read all about it! Fifty people swindled! Fifty people swindled!"

A curious man walked over and bought a paper. He checked the front page. He started to page through the paper. Then he growled at the paper boy.

"There's nothing here about fifty people being swindled!"

The paper boy kept yelling:

"Fifty-one people swindled! Read all about it!"

M-8

*****

Two golfers were chatting on the practice green, when one of them looked up and saw two women walking toward them.

One of them said, "Oh crap. Here comes my wife with some old witch she met in the clubhouse."

The other guy looked up and said, "Hey, mine too!"

M-9

*****

Abe and Esther are flying to Hawaii for a two week vacation to celebrate their 40th anniversary.

Suddenly, the Captain announces, "Ladies and Gentlemen, I am afraid I have some very bad news. Our engines have ceased functioning and we will attempt an emergency landing. Luckily, I see an uncharted island below us and we should be able to land on the beach. However, the odds are that we may never be rescued and will have to live on the island for the rest of our lives!"

Thanks to the skill of the flight crew, the plane lands safely on the island.

An hour later, sitting on the beach Abe turns to his wife and asks,

"Did you remember to send checks for the Visa and MasterCard this month?" he asks.

"Oh, forgive me, Abie," begged Esther. "I forgot."

Abe grabs her and gives her the biggest kiss in 40 years.

Esther pulls away and asks him, "What was that for?"

"They'll find us!"

M-10

*****

A young woman was having a physical examination and was embarrassed because of a weight problem. As she removed her last bit of clothing, she blushed. "I'm so ashamed, Doctor," she said, "I guess I let myself go."

The physician was checking hers eyes and ears. "Don't feel ashamed, Miss. You don't look that bad."

"Do you really think so, Doctor?" she asked.

The doctor held a tongue depressor in front of her face and said, "Of course. Now just open your mouth and say moo."

M-11

*****

A father sends a small boy to bed. Five minutes later….

"Da-ad…."

"What?"

"I'm thirsty. Can you bring drink of water?"

"No. You had your chance. Lights out."

Five minutes later: "Da-aaaad….."

"WHAT?"

"I'm THIRSTY. Can I have a drink of water??"

"I told you NO!" If you ask again, I'll have to spank you!!"

Five minutes later……"Daaaa-aaaad….."

"WHAT!"

"When you come in to spank me, can you bring a drink of water?"

M-12

*****

A History professor was explaining how society's ideal of beauty changes with time.

"Take Miss America in 1921," he noted. "She stood 5'1", weighed 108 pounds, and had measurements of 30-25-32. How do you think she'd do in today's beauty contest?"

One student piped up, "Not very well! She'd be way too old!"

M-13

*****

A woman on a west bound train asked the porter:

"Does this train stop in Los Angeles?"

The porter answered,

"If it doesn't, there's going to be a big splash!"

M-14

*****

A tramp knocked on the door of the inn known as St. George and the Dragon. The landlady answered the door.

The tramp said, “Could you give a poor man something to eat?”

“No,” said the woman, slamming the door in his face.

He knocked again and said, “Could I have a few words with St. George this time?”

M-15

*****

A really bad actor joins a traveling Shakespearian company.

They open with their first show in Chicago. As this bad actor starts Hamlet’s first speech, the audience starts to grumble and there are a few hisses and boos.

The actor tries to continue, but people start to shout insults, begging for the awful acting to stop. But the actor continues.

By now people are looking for garbage to throw at the actor. Finally the actor loses his concentration and turns on the audience.

“What do you want from me?” He screams. “I didn’t write this crap!”

M-16

*****

A man who attended no church suddenly develops a vague religious urge and decides to join a church—any church. So he sets out to find one.

His first stop is a Roman Catholic Church where he asks what he has to do to join. The priest mentions diligent study and the affirmation of the Nicene and Apostles' Creeds, then—just to see how much the man knows—asks him where Jesus was born.

“Pittsburgh,” he answers.

“Get out!” cries the shocked priest.

Next stop is a Southern Baptist church where the seeker is told he would have to learn Bible verses, swear belief in the Nicene and Apostles' creeds, swear off booze, and be baptized. The Baptist preacher then, to see how much this man knows, asks him where Jesus was born. “Philadelphia?” he asks tentatively.

“Get out, you heathen!” yells the preacher.

The man finally walks into a Unitarian church where he is told all he has to do is sign a membership card. “You mean I don't have to renounce anything, swear to anything, or be dunked in anything?”

“That's right. We have no special tests for membership, no dogma. We support total individual freedom of belief.”

“Then I'll join! But tell me—where was Jesus born?”

“Why, Bethlehem, of course.”

The man's face lights up. “I knew it was some place in Pennsylvania!”

M-17

*****

A lady is terribly overweight, so her doctor puts her on a diet. “I want you to eat regularly for 2 days, then skip the third day, eat regularly for two days, and then skip the third day, and repeat this procedure for 2 weeks. The next time I see you, you'll have lost at least 5 pounds.”

When the lady returned, she shocked the doctor by losing nearly 20 pounds.

“Why, that's amazing!” the doctor said, “Did you follow my instructions?”

The lady nodded… “I'll tell you though, I thought I was going to drop dead that 3rd day.”

“From hunger, you mean?” Asked the doctor.”

“No, from skipping.”

M-18

*****

A bum was walking down the street wearing only one shoe. A guy passing him asked:

“Did you lose a shoe?”

The bum answered:

“Nope. I found one.”

M-19

*****

Last year my wife and I toasted the New Year.

I had sourdough and she had whole wheat.

M-20

*****

One day two older ladies walked into an ice cream shop. One lady said, “two vanilla cones please!”

The cashier said, “Ok,” started making the cones for them and asked, “are you two sisters?”

They chuckled and replied, “No, we aren't even Catholic.”

M-21

*****

Two old friends were sitting on a park bench looking at the beautiful trees. One man said,

“You know, Joe, life is like a tree.”

The other man said,

“Why is life like a tree?”

The first man said, “How should I know? I’m not a philosopher.”

M-22

*****

Worried that they hadn't heard anything for days from the widow in the apartment next door, the mother said to her son, “Tony, would you go next door and see how old Mrs. Pierpoint is?”

A few minutes later, Tony returned.

“Well, is she all right?” asked the mother.

“She's fine, but you offended her,” remarked Tony.

“What did I do?” the mother exclaimed.

Tony replied, “Mrs. Pierpoint said it's none of your business how old she is.”

M-23

*****

A dietitian was once addressing a large audience in Chicago. “The material we put into our stomachs is enough to have killed most of us sitting here, years ago. Red meat is awful. Soft drinks erode your stomach lining. Chinese food is loaded with MSG, and none of us realizes the long-term harm caused by the germs in our drinking water.”

"But there is one thing that is the most dangerous of all and we all have, or will, eat it. Can anyone here tell me what food it is that causes the most grief and suffering for years after eating it?"

A 75-year-old man in the front row stood up and said,

"Wedding cake."

M-24

*****

An old lady was standing by the coffin at a funeral. She stepped tearfully up to the widow.

"Oh dear," she said, "I hope he didn't die of anything serious.

M-25

*****

The man told his doctor that he wasn't able to do all the things around the house that he used to do. The doctor started a long and thorough examination, but finally found nothing wrong with the man.

When the examination was complete, he said, "Now, Doc, I can take it. Tell me in plain English what is wrong with me."

"Well, in plain English," the doctor replied, "you're just lazy."

"Okay," said the man. "Now give me the medical term so I can tell my wife".

M-26

*****

When Marge discovered she was pregnant, she told her husband. Overjoyed, he said he'd buy her a new car.

For nine months, Marge went through morning sickness, discomfort, feelings of ugliness, and eventually a difficult labor and delivery. Lying in the recovery room, she said to another new mother:

"This is a hell of a way to get a new minivan."

M-27

*****

Two friends meet at the train station.

The first tells the second that he's on his way to Florida for his honeymoon.

"Congratulations!" exclaims the second friend. "But where's your wife?"

"Oh, she's already been to Florida."

M-28

*****

A woman brought an old book to an antique dealer to see if it was worth any money. The dealer examined the book carefully and became very excited.

"This is a rare find! It's a Gutenberg Bible. It's worth a fortune!"

The woman answered,

"Actually I had two of them. But I had to throw the other one in the trash. Some guy named Martin Luther had written all over it."

M-29

*****

A woman complained to her therapist.

"My daughter in law drives me crazy. She's always trying to push her way into our family. Even on the day my son got married, she wanted to be in all the wedding pictures."

M-30

*****

My wife: I fell into a large vat of milk today and almost drowned!

Me: Pasteurized?

My wife: No, just up to my neck.

We haven't talked about puns in this book. Puns are a different subject. But just in case you're wondering, this joke is a good one.

M-31

*****

A man showed up to late to work. His angry boss asked him,

"What happened?"

The man answered, "The alarm clock woke everybody but me!"

The boss shook his head. "How could that happen?"

"Well, it was set for six, and there are seven of us in the house."

M-32

*****

A man calls the front desk from room 1248 in a hotel. He asks to be transferred to maintenance.

“What’s the problem there?” asks the clerk.

“My wife has gone berserk and is threatening to jump out the window.”

The clerk tells him that this is a police matter, not a maintenance issue.

“Well, she can’t get the window open, and that’s a maintenance problem.”

M-33

*****

A meek little man walked into the butcher and called to the lady behind the counter.

Woman: Yes?

Meek-Sounding Man: Pardon me, do you have any raw beefsteak?

Woman: What do you need it for?

Meek-Sounding Man: Well, my wife tried to chase a dog out of our yard. She stepped on a rake and it gave her a black eye.

Woman: Oh dear! Well, ice is better for a black eye, you know.

Meek-Sounding Man: Oh, it's not for my wife. It's for the dog, bless his heart!

M-34

*****

While visiting family in the south a lady had ordered dinner in a restaurant. Her salad arrived with an orange dressing, and she called the waitress over. After looking the situation over, the waitress said:

"Oh I'm sorry, hon. You must have said 'ranch', and I thought you said, 'franch'.

M-35

*****

A famous artist was at the height of her career when she began losing her eyesight. She went to a very famous eye doctor for treatment. After a delicate surgery, her eyes began heal and her eyesight improved.

As a demonstration of her thanks, the artist when to the doctor's office and painted a gigantic eye on the wall of the doctor's waiting room.

The press caught wind of the story and wanted to interview the doctor.

"How does this lovely painting in your office make you feel?"

The doctor rubbed his chin and raised an eyebrow.

"It makes me thankful I'm not a gynecologist."

M-36

*****

A man from Kansas City was trying to locate an old high school friend who had been living for a few years in Detroit. He called directory assistance. He waited for a minute while the operator searched for the listing.

"Your friend has quite a common name. I'll need more information. Do you have a street name?"

"Ah," stammered the man, "Some of my friends call me 'the iceman'.

M-37

*****

A woman went to a psychiatrist because she had gained a lot of weight. Because she had become so obese, she didn't like to go out much, and her friends had started to comment on her size and her pale complexion.

"My self esteem is at an all time low, can you help me doctor?"

The psychiatrist wrote on his pad and nodded.

"Now, I need to ask you to go over there by the window, and lie on the floor."

The woman did as the doctor directed. He nodded and went on.

"And now, please go lie in front of that bookcase."

The woman moved to the new location and arranged herself on the floor.

"And finally, please go lie on the floor next to the door."

The woman stretched out on the floor next to the door and the doctor went back to writing on his notepad.

"You can have a seat on this chair now."

The woman watched the doctor write and asked him:

"Do you think you can help me, Doctor?"

"No, but here's a prescription for some pills that will calm you."

The lady took the prescription with confusion on her face.

"What was all that lying on the floor about?"

"Oh, I just bought a white couch and I'm trying to figure out where it would look best."

Chapter Twelve

SLAP STICK COMEDY

"Slap-stick comedy is really funny, unless you're the one getting slapped with the stick."

Lots of people think that "funny" means someone falling down, or one person hitting another, or other kinds of physical misfortunes.

I've seen lots of slap stick pranks that really made me laugh, but you need to understand that there is much more to humor than someone falling down.

I personally know people who will sit stone-faced through a good comedy routine, and then laugh themselves silly during a fight scene in a movie that was not intended to be funny.

The problem I see with an unhealthy obsession with slap stick is the idea that other people's pain is funny. It's a lot like sarcasm and insults.

On the other hand, slapstick comedy is a classic form of humor, and there is much to be learned from slapstick about timing and delivery.

Slapstick comedy is also a form of observational comedy, like cartoons. Slapstick comedy often involves impeccable timing. Watch the Three Stooges and see how amazingly choreographed their comedy routines are.

Visual comedy, like cartoons and slapstick, teach us the importance of context. We all understand how funny the "pie in the face" is. The context is very important. Surprise, anticipation, revenge. The humor of the situation can build and build.

CHAPTER THIRTEEN

KIDS JOKES

So, kid's jokes are kind of silly. But don't discount them, because we can learn a lot from kid's jokes.

Kid's jokes are simple and to the point.

Kids love jokes that are ridiculous and don't make sense. That's a lesson we shouldn't forget.

1. What is a forum? - Two-um plus two-um!
2. "Johnny, why did you kick your brother in the stomach?" exclaimed the angry mother. "It was pure accident, Mama. He turned around."
3. Q: What says "Eoo?" A: A cow with no lips.
4. How did Columbus's men sleep on their ships? - With their eyes shut!
5. Who invented fractions? - Henry the 1/8th!
6. Where was the Declaration of Independence signed? - At the bottom!
7. Teacher: Now class, whatever I ask, I want you to all answer together.

   How much is six plus 4?

   Class: Together!
8. Where did the pilgrims land when they came to America? - On their feet!
9. Teacher: That's quite a cough you have there, what are you taking for it?

   Pupil: I don't know teacher. What will you give me?

10. I failed every subject except for algebra.

    How did you keep from failing that?

    I didn't take algebra!

11. Teacher: When was Rome built?

    Pupil: At night.

    Teacher: Why did you say that?

    Pupil: Because my Dad always says that Rome wasn't built in a day!

12. Q: What did one toilet say to the other toilet?

    A: You look a bit flushed.

13. Teacher: What's big and yellow and comes in the morning to brighten a mothers day?

    Pupil: The school bus!

14. Teacher: You missed school yesterday didn't you? - Pupil: Not very much!

15. Who designed Noah's ark? - An ark-itect!

16. Why was George Washington buried at Mount Vernon? - Because he was dead!

17. Teacher: Can anyone tell me how many seconds there are in a year?

    Pupil: 12 - 2nd January, 2nd February…!

18. Mother: What did you learn in school today?

    Son: How to write

    Mother: What did you write?

    Son: I don't know, they haven't taught us how to read yet!

19. What's yellow, has wheels and lies on its back? - A dead school bus!

20. What's a mushroom? - The place they store the school food!

21. Teacher: What can you tell me about the Dead Sea?

    Pupil: Dead?, I didn't even know he was sick!

22. What are you going to be when you get out of school? - An old man!

23. What did you learn in school today? - Not enough, I have to go back tomorrow!

24. Pupil: I don't think I deserved zero on this test!

    Teacher: I agree, but that's the lowest mark I could give you!

25. What do you call a pig that knows karate? - A pork chop!

26. Why do bees have sticky hair? -Because they use honeycombs.

27. Why was the man running around his bed? -He wanted to catch up on his sleep.

28. Why is 6 afraid of 7? -Because 7 8 9!

29. What's black and white, black and white, black and white? -A penguin rolling down a hill!

30. Why do cows wear bells? -Because their horns don't work!

31. What does a snail say when it's riding on a turtle's back? -Weeeee!!

32. What is brown and sticky? -A stick!

33. What's mom and dad's favorite ride at a fair? - A married-go-round!

34. What do you call a monkey in a mine field? A baboom.

35. A Glacier was asked what it thought about global warming.

    It replied, “To tell you the truth, I've never really thawed about it.”

36. How do you get to be a good wood carver?

    Whittle by Whittle

37. What do you call a dog that does magic tricks?

    A Labracadabrador.

38. Why is Cinderella never any good at soccer?

    Because she is always running away from the ball.

39. Why can't you hear a pterodactyl going to the bathroom?

    Because the “P” is silent.

40. Where do you go to learn how to make banana splits?

    Sundae School

41. What is the difference between boogers and broccoli?

    Kids won't eat their broccoli!

42. Q: Why did the elephant sit on the marshmallow?

    A: So he wouldn't fall into the hot chocolate.

43. Why don't people fart in church?

    Because they would have to sit in their own pew.

44. A chicken and a duck are standing on the road side, and the chicken says to the duck:

    "Buddy, don't cross this road, or you'll never hear the end of it."

45. Q. What's faster, hot or cold? A. Hot, because you can catch a cold.

46. How do you kill a circus? Go for the juggler.

47. What do you call nose without a body? No body nose!

48. What do you find in a clean nose? Finger prints.

49. What did one casket say to the other casket? Is that you coughin?

50. Q: Did you hear about the kidnapping at school?

    A: It's okay. He woke up.

51. Q: What do Alexander the Great and Kermit the Frog have in common?

    A: Their middle names

52. What goes moof? A cow with buck teeth.

53. In a Classroom the teacher asks; Maria, go to the map and find North America

    MARIA: Here it is.

    TEACHER: Correct. Now class, who discovered America?

    CLASS: Maria.

54. Did you hear about the giant with diarrhea? A: You didn't? It's all over town.

55. "What happens to liars when they die?" Answer - "They lie still."

56. 'Why did the pig stop sunbathing? He was bacon in the heat.'

57. Q: What do you call someone who doesn't fart in public? A: A private tooter.

58. Where do caveman store their weapons? In the clubhouse

59. If we get rid of all the margarine the world will be a butter place.

60. Why can't you hear a pterodactyl go to the bathroom? Because the "P" is silent.

61. When you get a bladder infection, urine trouble.

62. Where are average things made? In the satisfactory.

63. The other day I held the door open for a clown. I thought it was a nice jester.

CHAPTER FOURTEEN

ONE-LINERS

One-liners are a joke-teller's best friend. They are easy to memorize, and can be pulled out and tossed at an audience at the drop of a hat. They catch people off-guard.

Sometimes you just have a moment to be funny. Maybe there's just a sudden lull in the conversation. These jokes can be thrown in quickly and everyone will laugh!

These are also perfect "tie in" jokes. These are the jokes you should put on your recipe cards. Reference them by subject. You'll be amazed at the result when you throw these jokes out there.

Following are some great one-liners:

1. People say that money is not the key to happiness...But I always figured if you have enough money, you can have a key made.
2. When is the only time you're justified in slapping your mother-in-law in the mouth?

   When her mustache is on fire.
3. How Do Crazy People Go Through The Forest? They Take The Psycho Path
4. How Do You Get Holy Water? You Boil The Hell Out Of It.
5. What Do Fish Say When They Hit a Concrete Wall? Dam!
6. What Do Eskimos Get From Sitting On The Ice too Long? Polaroid's
7. What Do You Call a Boomerang That Doesn't work? A Stick
8. What Do You Call Cheese That Isn't Yours? Nacho Cheese.

9. What Do You Call Santa's Helpers? Subordinate Clauses.
10. What Do You Call Four Bullfighters In Quicksand?

    Quattro Sinko.
11. What Do You Get from a Pampered Cow? Spoiled Milk.
12. What Do You Get When You Cross a Snowman With a Vampire?

    Frostbite.
13. What Lies At The Bottom Of The Ocean And Twitches?

    A Nervous Wreck
14. What's The Difference Between Roast Beef And Pea Soup?

    Anyone Can Roast Beef.
15. Where Do You Find a Dog With No Legs?

    Right Where You Left Him.
16. Why Do Gorillas Have Big Nostrils? Because They Have Big Fingers.
17. Why Don't Blind People Like To Sky Dive?

    Because It Scares The Dog.
18. What Kind Of Coffee Was Served On The Titanic? Sanka.
19. Why Did Pilgrims' Pants Always Fall Down?

    Because They Wore Their Belt Buckle On Their Hat.
20. What's The Difference Between a Bad Golfer And a Bad Skydiver?

    A Bad Golfer Goes, Whack, Dang!

    A Bad Skydiver Goes Dang! Whack.
21. How are a Texas tornado and a Tennessee divorce the same?

    Somebody's gonna lose a trailer.
22. Follow your dreams, except for that one where you're naked at work.

23. I asked God for a bike, but I know God doesn't work that way. So I stole a bike and asked for forgiveness.
24. If 4 out of 5 people SUFFER from diarrhea… does that mean that one enjoys it?
25. Some people are like Slinkies … not really good for anything, but you can't help smiling when you see one tumble down the stairs.
26. My friend has kleptomania, but when it gets bad, he takes something for it.
27. When everything's coming your way, you're in the wrong lane.
28. Two wrongs don't make a right, but two Wrights make an airplane.
29. When the chips are down, the buffalo is empty.
30. I got a sweater for Christmas. What I really wanted was a screamer or a moaner.
31. My short-term memory is not as sharp as it used to be. Also, my short-term memory's not as sharp as it used to be.
32. Which is worse, Ignorance or Apathy? I don't know and I don't care.
33. Getting on a plane, I told the ticket lady, "Send one of my bags to New York, send one to Los Angeles, and send one to Miami." She said, "We can't do that!" I told her, "You did it last week!"
34. My girlfriend told me I should be more affectionate. So I got two girlfriends.
35. I was standing there wondering: Why does a Frisbee appear larger the closer it gets? And then it hit me.
36. My wife and I have decided we don't want children. If anyone does, we can drop them off tomorrow.
37. My wife was abducted by MIMES…they did UNSPEAKABLE things to her.
38. I like what mechanics wear, , over all.

39. I quit my job at the helium gas factory. I refuse to be spoken to in that tone!
40. In college I was going to join the debate team, but someone talked me out of it.
41. My dentist was voted 'Dentist Of The Year'. He didn't get a trophy, they just gave him a little plaque.
42. My uncle died when he was crushed by a piano. His funeral was very low keyed.
43. I was involved in blind date that went horribly wrong. We've been married for ten years now.
44. They say that opposites attract, but try explaining that to my ugly wife.
45. Grandpa always said when one door closes, another one opens. Great man, horrible cabinet maker.
46. Customer: Waiter, I'm in a hurry! Will the pancakes be long?

    Waiter: No sir, round.
47. Money-wise I'm set for life, provided I die next Tuesday.
48. I'd kill for a Nobel Peace Prize
49. A man walks in to a grocery store and asks, "Do you have helicopter flavored chips?"

    "Nope," says the clerk. "Just plane ones."
50. How did Captain Hook die? Jock itch.
51. Q: How does a crazy guy get through the forest?

    A: He takes the psychopath.
52. Q: What is E.T. short for?

    A: Coz he's got little legs
53. What did the scarf say to the hat? You go on a head, I'll just hang around.
54. What's orange and sounds like a Parrot? A Carrot!

55. **Q**: How many Spaniards does it take to screw in a light bulb?

    A: Juan.

56. My mom has become addicted to watching "Dancing with the Stars".

    We're forcing her to enroll in a two-step program.

57. Did you hear about the cannibal who passed his brother in the forest?

58. What d'you do when you see a spaceman? Park in it dude!

59. Skeleton walks into a bar and says, "Gimme a beer and a mop."

60. How many dull people does it take to change a light bulb? One.

61. What does one half of a loaf of bread look like? The other half

62. Q. What's grey? A. A melted penguin.

63. Where do you find a dog with no legs? Right where you left him.

64. Did you hear the one about the three holes in the ground? Well, well, well…

65. Q: how much did the pirate pay for his peg leg and hook? A: An arm and a leg

66. Mom: "Don't play with boys, they're too rough."

    Daughter: "What if I find a smooth one?"

67. Two peanuts are walking down the street. One was assaulted.

68. What do you call a fish with no eye? FSH

69. What do you call a deer with no eyes? I have no eye deer.

70. A computer once beat me at chess, but it was no match for me at kick boxing.

71. Quit worrying about your health. It'll go away.

72. Constipated people don't give a crap.

73. What do you call someone who puts poison in a person's corn flakes? A cereal killer

74. I could lend a hand, but I prefer to give a finger
75. Anyone who says an onion is the only vegetable that will make you cry has never been hit in the face with a pumpkin.
76. Employee of the month is a good example of how somebody can be both a winner and a loser at the same time.
77. A pessimist is someone who looks at the land of milk and honey and sees only calories and cholesterol
78. Time is a great teacher, but unfortunately it kills all its pupils.
79. My neighbor asked if he could use my lawnmower. I told him of course he could, as long as he didn't take it out of my yard.
80. An egotist is someone who is usually me-deep in conversation.
81. What's the best side of the cemetery to live on? The outside.
82. Show me a guy with a few drinks under his belt and I'll show you a guy with soggy shorts.
83. Never lie to an x-ray technician. They can see right through you.
84. When I asked you for a flower, you gave me a garden… When I asked you for a stone, you gave me a statue… What are you… deaf?
85. Doctors tell us there are over seven million people who are overweight. These, of course, are only round figures.
86. Change is good as long as I don't have to do anything different
87. When someone says. "It tastes like crap." ….how do they know?
88. My friend works at a police station doing sketches of suspects. He's a con artist.
89. A bird in the hand is the best way to eat chicken.
90. Where do you get virgin wool? From ugly sheep
91. With great power comes a great electric bill.
92. Police officer: Excuse me, but your dog has been chasing a man on his bicycle.

    Dog owner: Are you crazy? My dog can't even ride a bicycle.

93. It takes two bureaucrats to screw in a lightbulb. One to insert it and one to screw it up.

94. If you put on a clean pair of socks every morning, by the end of the week you won't be able to get your shoes on.

95. What kind of sword is only used by women? A broadsword.

96. I went to see a urologist and he said that I could go at any time.

97. What word is always pronounced wrong? Wrong!

98. One arm butlers – they can take it but they can't dish it out…

99. A Husband accidentally sent this to his wife, "I'm having a wonderful time, wish you were her."

100. Apparently, California has the highest rate of Adultery and Depression. It's a sad State of affairs

101. The best thing about telepathy is…I know, right?

102. How about a cat joke? Just kitten.

103. I wrote a book about reverse psychology… You wouldn't like it.

104. I could snap at any moment. Seriously, with either hand.

105. Teach a child to be polite and courteous, and when he grows up, he'll never be able to change lanes on the freeway.

106. Girl: "I can't be your valentine for medical reasons."

Boy: "Really?" Girl: "Yeah, you make me sick!"

107. A jumper cable walks into a bar. The bartender says,

"I'll serve you, but don't start anything."

108. Two aerial antennas meet on a roof, fall in love and get married.

The ceremony wasn't much, but the reception was excellent.

109. Good news for insomniacs! Only three more sleeps til Christmas!

110. What do a mole and an eagle have in common?

They both live underground, except the eagle.

111. I went to buy some camouflage trousers the other day but I couldn't find any.

112. As the dog said when he got his tail caught in the lawn mower, It won't be long now.

113. Last month I went on a Once-in-a-lifetime vacation trip. I'll tell you what, never again!

114. When I was a kid they made me walk the plank. We couldn't afford a dog.

115. My uncle Bob drowned. For his funeral we got him a wreath shaped like a like preserver. It's what he would have wanted.

116. They held a beauty contest in my hometown, and nobody won.

117. How many surrealists does it take to screw in a light bulb? A fish.

118. Did you hear about the man who got cooled to absolute zero? He's 0-K now.

119. There are two types of people in the world: Those who crave closure

120. There are two types of people in the world: Those who can extrapolate from incomplete data sets

121. It's hard to explain puns to kleptomaniacs because they always take things literally.

122. The sign in front of the drug rehab center said, "keep off the grass."

123. All I ask is the chance to prove that money can't make me happy.

124. I have either gained a few pounds or there is a bowl of Jell-o following me.

125. How dare you incinerate that I'm bad with big words?

126. Q: When driving through fog, what should you use?

A: Your steering wheel.

127. Q: What is the difference between a flashing red traffic light and a flashing yellow traffic light?

 A: The color.

128. My boss says he's going to fire the employee with the worst posture.

 I've got a hunch it might be me.

129. How does a rich girl change a light bulb? She says: Daddy I want a new apartment!

130. I broke up with my cross-eyed girlfriend. I thought she was seeing someone else.

131. What did the farmer say when he lost his tractor? Where's my tractor?

132. There are two reasons I don't drink out of the toilet: Number 1 and Number 2.

133. I'm getting my wife a mirror for her birthday. That'll show her who's the boss.

134. Ignorant? I don't know the meaning of the word!

135. If I'm ignorant, this is the first I'm hearing of it.

136. I hate it when a sentence doesn't turn out the way you think it kangaroo.

137. Love means nothing to a tennis player.

138. In England they call it the lift. Here in America we call it the elevator. I guess we're just raised differently.

139. How to wash dishes. 1. Put dirty dishes in the sink. 2. Wait.

140. Selfish: What the owner of a sea food store does.

141. I showed up at a fancy dress party dressed as a football. I was immediately kicked out.

142. I fell off a fifty-foot ladder today. Luckily I was on the bottom step.

143. Danger is my middle name. First name: Avoids. Last name: Completely.

144. I accidentally gave my girlfriend a glue stick instead of chapstick. She's still not talking to me.

145. A lot of money is tainted. 'Taint yours and 'taint mine.

150. I looked through a book called "50 things to do before you die".

I was sure that "shout for help" would be one of them.

151. When you've seen one shopping center you've seen a mall.

152. The thief who stole our calendar got twelve months.

153. Eighty percent of men cheat in America. The rest cheat in Europe.

154. I'm going to stand outside. So if anyone asks, I am outstanding.

155. Never anthropomorphize computers. They hate that.

156. What did the worms say when they buried the preacher?

"Ymmm, Divinity!

157. Q. Where did Napoleon keep his armies? A. In his sleevies!

158. You know what I find odd? Numbers that can't be divided by 2.

159. I ate four large cans of alphabet soup and it caused me to have a large vowel movement.

160. How many lawyers does it take to screw in a light bulb?

One, but boy, does it get screwed!

161. Q: What do you call a poodle that gets run over by a truck? A: A puddle.

162. My doctor told me to drink a glass of wine after a hot bath, but I could never finish drinking the hot bath.

163. My wife asked me to whisper something soft and sweet in her her, so I said: "chocolate fudge".

164. A Spanish speaking magician told the audience he'll disappear on the count of three.

He said "Uno, dos", *POOF*. He disappeared without a tres.

165. I feel like a tap dancer in the canoe of life.

166. Last night me and my wife watched three DVDs back to back. Luckily I was the one facing the television.

167. How did they know the man eaten by the shark had dandruff? They found his head and shoulders on the beach.

168. Our town is so small we had to shoot a visitor to start a cemetary.

169. I like to walk into crematoriums and say, "What's cooking?"

170. How many musicians does it take to screw in a lightbulb? A: One, two, one, two, three, four!

171. I guess surrealism isn't my cup of tuna.

172. I had a fight with my shoe laces this morning. It ended up in a tie.

173. I dig, you dig, we dig, he dig, she dig, they dig....

Its not a beautiful poem, but its very deep

174. My friend recently got crushed by a pile of books.

He's only got his shelf to blame.

175. Pediatricians tend to have very little patients.

176. Why do chicken coops have two doors? Because if they had four doors, they'd be chicken sedans.

177. If I had to choose between pancakes and French toast, I'd waffle.

178. Flying in a plane can be a bumpy ride, even while taxiing on the ground. But it's not the pilot's fault. It's not the airline's fault. It's the asphalt.

179. "I'm sorry" and "I apologize" mean the same thing... except when you're at a funeral.

180. I saw a couple drive past in a car that had the words "just married" painted on it. I stopped them and said, "You're more than that."

181. My wife told me romance is better when you're on vacation. That wasn't a very nice postcard to receive.

182. The only time incorrectly isn't spelled incorrectly is when it's spelled incorrectly.

183. I'll stop at nothing to avoid using negative numbers.

184. My friend watched a Batman DVD with a girl on their 9th date. It went "dinner dinner dinner dinner dinner dinner dinner dinner BATMAN.

185. Remember, it doesn't matter if you're rich or poor, as long as you've got money.

186. I smashed open my piggy bank earlier. I've got just about enough in it to buy a new piggy bank.

187. I ordered venison stew at the diner. It was five bucks.

188. It's impossible to carry a watermelon without seeming proud or ashamed of it.

189. "Pickup artists" and "garbage men" should switch names.

190. To whoever stole my antidepressants, I hope you're happy now!

191. I like a warm toilet seat, except when it's a public bathroom.

192. My doctor wants me to change my eating habits and try vegetarianism.

But I'm not sure I can give up cold turkey.